British and American Essays
1905-1956

# British and American

# ESSAYS

## 1905=1956

*Compiled by*

CARL L. ANDERSON

AND

GEORGE WALTON WILLIAMS

DUKE UNIVERSITY

**Holt, Rinehart and Winston**
New York — Chicago — San Francisco
Toronto — London

# Acknowledgments

The editors are grateful to the following persons and firms for permission to reprint:

"A Piece of Chalk" from Tremendous Trifles by G. K. Chesterton. Reprinted by permission of Miss Dorothy Collins, Methuen & Co., Ltd., and Sheed and Ward, Inc. Copyright 1909.

"Christs in the Tirol" from Phoenix by D. H. Lawrence, included in The Viking Portable D. H. Lawrence. Copyright 1936 by Frieda Lawrence. Reprinted by permission of The Viking Press, Inc., and the Estate of the late Mrs. Frieda Lawrence.

"Outside Literature" from Last Essays by Joseph Conrad. Reprinted by permission of J. M. Dent & Sons Ltd.

"A Lost Wood" from Out of Soundings by H. M. Tomlinson. Reprinted by permission of The Society of Authors as the literary representative of the Estate of the late H. M. Tomlinson.

"A Sentimental Journey" by Ivor Brown, reprinted by permission of the author.

"My Wood" from Abinger Harvest, copyright 1936 by E. M. Forster. Reprinted by permission of Edward Arnold (Publishers) Ltd. and Harcourt, Brace and Company, Inc.

"In Praise of Ignorance," reprinted from A Conversation with a Cat and Others by Hilaire Belloc by permission of Cassell and Company, Ltd.

"The Calamity of Appomattox" reprinted from A Mencken Chrestomathy by H. L. Mencken, by permission of Alfred A. Knopf, Inc. Copyright 1949 by Alfred A. Knopf, Inc.

"Seed Corn and Mistletoe" by Bernard DeVoto, reprinted by permission of Mrs. Bernard DeVoto.

"Sex ex Machina" by James Thurber, reprinted by permission of the author. Copyright © 1937 The New Yorker Magazine, Inc.

"Once More to the Lake" from One Man's Meat by E. B. White. Copyright 1941 by E. B. White. Reprinted by permission of Harper & Brothers and Victor Gollancz Ltd.

"The Death of the Moth" from The Death of the Moth and Other Essays by Virginia Woolf, copyright, 1942, by Harcourt, Brace and Company, Inc. Reprinted by permission of the publishers and Leonard Woolf.

"The Country of the Blind" from *Season in the Sun and Other Pleasures* by Wolcott Gibbs. Copyright 1945 by Wolcott Gibbs. Reprinted by permission of *The Saturday Review* and Random House, Inc.

"Some Thoughts on the Common Toad" from *Shooting an Elephant and Other Essays* by George Orwell, copyright 1945, 1946, 1949, 1950 by Sonia Brownell Orwell. Reprinted by permission of Harcourt, Brace and Company, Inc., and Martin Secker & Warburg Ltd.

"Out of a Book" reprinted from *Collected Impressions* by Elizabeth Bowen, by permission of Alfred A. Knopf, Inc., and the author. Published 1950 by Alfred A. Knopf, Inc.

"The Meaning of Treason" from *The Meaning of Treason* by Rebecca West, as originally published in *Harper's* (October 1947). Copyright 1947 by Rebecca West. Reprinted by permission of The Viking Press, Inc., and Macmillan and Company, Ltd.

"The Future Is Now," copyright, 1950, by Katherine Anne Porter. Reprinted from her volume, *The Days Before*, by permission of Harcourt, Brace and Company, Inc.

"A Visit to America" from *Quite Early One Morning* by Dylan Thomas. Copyright 1954 by New Directions. Reprinted by permission of New Directions and J. M. Dent & Sons Ltd.

"On Education" from *Thoughts in the Wilderness* by J. B. Priestley. Copyright © 1957 by J. B. Priestley. Reprinted by permission of Harper & Brothers and William Heinemann Ltd.

"Televiewing" from *Thoughts in the Wilderness* by J. B. Priestley. Copyright © 1957 by J. B. Priestley. Reprinted by permission of Harper & Brothers and William Heinemann Ltd.

# Preface

The essays in this book have been selected on the basis of literary excellence and diversity of subject. They are the personal utterances of writers who have mastered their art, and they share with other forms of creative literature the power to move, to stimulate, and to please through beauty and wit in the use of language. They were written as essays, not as topical magazine articles or chapters in books, and they are all reprinted in their entirety. Like the essays of an earlier time, they discover in seemingly trivial or commonplace subjects profoundly significant themes and ideas.

We wish to acknowledge with special thanks the assistance of Professor Francis E. Bowman, our colleagues, and the reference staff of the Duke University Library.

C. L. A.
G. W. W.

Durham, North Carolina
June, 1959

# Contents

# A PIECE OF CHALK

## G. K. *Chesterton*

G. K. Chesterton (1874-1936), born and educated in England, was trained first as a draftsman and artist, but before he was twenty-one he had established himself as a journalist, reviewer, and essayist. From 1905 to 1930 he supplied a weekly essay to The Illustrated London News and at the same time wrote for many other journals. His "Father Brown" detective stories form some of this output. A devout Roman Catholic, he crusaded, especially in his later essays, for a wider understanding of the metaphysics and theology of his faith; even in this early essay some of this concern may be felt.

The essay appeared originally in the (London) Daily News (November 4, 1905) and is reprinted from Tremendous Trifles (1909).

I remember one splendid morning, all blue and silver, in the summer holidays when I reluctantly tore myself away from the task of doing nothing in particular, and put on a hat of some sort and picked up a walking-stick, and put six very bright-coloured chalks in my pocket. I then went into the kitchen (which, along with the rest of the house, belonged to a very square and sensible old woman in a Sussex village), and asked the owner and occupant of the kitchen if she had any brown paper. She had a great deal; in fact, she had too much; and she mistook the purpose and the rationale of the existence of brown paper. She seemed to have an idea that if a person wanted brown paper he must be wanting to tie up parcels; which was the last thing I wanted to do; indeed, it is a thing which I have found to be beyond my mental capacity. Hence she dwelt very much on the varying qualities of toughness and endurance in the material. I explained to her that I only wanted to draw pictures on it, and that I did not want them to endure in the least; and that from my point of view, therefore, it was a question, not of tough

1

consistency, but of responsive surface, a thing comparatively irrelevant in a parcel. When she understood that I wanted to draw she offered to overwhelm me with note-paper, apparently supposing that I did my notes and correspondence on old brown paper wrappers from motives of economy.

I then tried to explain the rather delicate logical shade, that I not only liked brown paper, but liked the quality of brownness in paper, just as I liked the quality of brownness in October woods, or in beer, or in the peat-streams of the North. Brown paper represents the primal twilight of the first toil of creation, and with a bright-coloured chalk or two you can pick out points of fire in it, sparks of gold, and blood-red, and sea-green, like the first fierce stars that sprang out of divine darkness. All this I said (in an off-hand way) to the old woman; and I put the brown paper in my pocket along with the chalks, and possibly other things. I suppose every one must have reflected how primeval and how poetical are the things that one carries in one's pocket; the pocket-knife, for instance, the type of all human tools, the infant of the sword. Once I planned to write a book of poems entirely about the things in my pockets. But I found it would be too long; and the age of the great epics is past.

With my stick and my knife, my chalks and my brown paper, I went out on to the great downs. I crawled across those colossal contours that express the best quality of England, because they are at the same time soft and strong. The smoothness of them has the same meaning as the smoothness of great cart-horses, or the smoothness of the beech-tree; it declares in the teeth of our timid and cruel theories that the mighty are merciful. As my eye swept the land-scape, the landscape was as kindly as any of its cottages, but for power it was like an earthquake. The villages in the immense valley were safe, one could see, for centuries; yet the lifting of the whole land was like the lifting of one enormous wave to wash them all away.

I crossed one swell of living turf after another, looking for a place to sit down and draw. Do not, for heaven's sake, imagine I was going to sketch from Nature. I was going to draw devils and seraphim, and blind old gods that men worshipped before the dawn of right, and saints in robes of angry crimson, and seas of strange green, and all the sacred or monstrous symbols that look so well in bright colours on brown paper. They are much better worth drawing than Nature; also they are much easier to draw. When a cow came slouching by in the field next to me, a mere artist might have drawn it; but I always get wrong in the hind legs of quadrupeds. So I drew the soul of the cow; which I saw there plainly walking before me in the sunlight; and the soul was all purple and silver, and had seven horns and the mystery that belongs to all the beasts. But though I could not with a crayon get the best out of the landscape, it does not follow that the landscape was not getting the best out of me. And this, I think, is the mistake that people make about the old poets who lived before Wordsworth, and were supposed not to care very much about Nature because they did not describe it much.

They preferred writing about great men to writing about great hills; but they sat on the great hills to write it. They gave out much less about Nature, but they drank in, perhaps, much more. They painted the white robes of their holy virgins with the blinding snow, at which they had stared all day. They blazoned the shields of their paladins with the purple and gold of many heraldic sunsets. The greenness of a thousand green leaves clustered into the live green figure of Robin Hood. The blueness of a score of forgotten skies became the blue robes of the Virgin. The inspiration went in like sunbeams and came out like Apollo.

But as I sat scrawling these silly figures on the brown paper, it began to dawn on me, to my great disgust, that I had left one chalk, and that a most exquisite and essential chalk, behind. I searched all my pockets, but I could not find any white chalk. Now, those who are acquainted with all the philosophy (nay, religion) which is typified in the art of drawing on brown paper, know that white is positive and essential. I cannot avoid remarking here upon a moral significance. One of the wise and awful truths which this brown-paper art reveals, is this, that white is a colour. It is not a mere absence of colour; it is a shining and affirmative thing, as fierce as red, as definite as black. When, so to speak, your pencil grows red-hot, it draws roses; when it grows white-hot, it draws stars. And one of the two or three defiant verities of the best religious morality, of real Christianity, for example, is exactly this same thing; the chief assertion of religious morality is that white is a colour. Virtue is not the absence of vices or the avoidance of moral dangers; virtue is a vivid and separate thing, like pain or a particular smell. Mercy does not mean not being cruel or sparing people revenge or punishment; it means a plain and positive thing like the sun, which one has either seen or not seen.

Chastity does not mean abstention from sexual wrong; it means something flaming, like Joan of Arc. In a word, God paints in many colours; but He never paints so gorgeously, I had almost said so gaudily, as when He paints in white. In a sense our age has realised this fact, and expressed it in our sullen costume. For if it were really true that white was a blank and colourless thing, negative and non-committal, then white would be used instead of black and grey for the funeral dress of this pessimistic period. We should see city gentlemen in frock coats of spotless silver linen, with top hats as white as wonderful arum lilies. Which is not the case.

Meanwhile, I could not find my chalk.

I sat on the hill in a sort of despair. There was no town nearer than Chichester at which it was even remotely probable that there would be such a thing as an artist's colourman. And yet, without white, my absurd little pictures would be as pointless as the world would be if there were no good people in it. I stared stupidly round, racking my brain for expedients. Then I suddenly stood up and roared with laughter, again and again, so that the cows stared at me and called a committee. Imagine a man in the Sahara regretting that he had no sand for his hour-glass. Imagine a gentleman in mid-ocean wishing that he had brought some salt water with him for his chemical experiments. I was sitting on an immense warehouse of white chalk. The landscape was made entirely out of white chalk. White chalk was piled more miles until it met the sky. I stooped and broke a piece off the rock I sat on: it did not mark so well as the shop chalks do; but it gave the effect. And I stood there in a trance of pleasure, realising that this Southern England is not only a grand peninsula, and a tradition and a civilisation; it is something even more admirable. It is a piece of chalk.

# CHRISTS IN THE TIROL

## D. H. Lawrence

D. H. Lawrence (1885-1930), the son of a Nottinghamshire
miner, is best known for his travel books and for his novels
in which he probes "the dark founts of creative life." In
August 1912 he began a walking tour from Austria through
the Brenner Pass to Lake Garda in Italy. His impression of
the wayside crucifixes is recorded in this essay.

The essay appeared originally in the Westminster Gazette
(1913), was extensively revised with a new title for Lawrence's
travel book, Twilight in Italy (1916), and was further revised
and published under its original title in Atlantic Monthly
(1933). The version given here follows the original of 1913,
reprinted in Phoenix: The Posthumous Papers of D. H.
Lawrence (1936).

The real Tirol does not seem to extend far south of the Brenner, and
northward it goes right to the Starnberger See. Even at Sterzing the
rather gloomy atmosphere of the Tirolese Alps is being dispersed by
the approach of the South. And, strangely enough, the roadside
crucifixes become less and less interesting after Sterzing. Walking
down from Munich to Italy, I have stood in front of hundreds of
Martertafeln;[1] and now I miss them; these painted shrines by the
Garda See are not the same.

I, who see a tragedy in every cow, began by suffering from the
Secession pictures [2] in Munich. All these new paintings seemed so
shrill and restless. Those that were meant for joy shrieked and
pranced for joy, and sorrow was a sensation to be relished, curiously;
as if we were epicures in suffering, keen on a new flavour. I thought

---

[1] Figures of the Passion erected along the roadside to mark places where wayfarers
have met with fatal accidents.

[2] Secession pictures were those painted by a group of art nouveau artists in
Austria (1890-1905) and considered at the time daring and advanced.

with kindliness of England, whose artists so often suck their sadness like a lollipop, mournfully, and comfortably.

Then one must walk, as it seems, for miles and endless miles past crucifixes, avenues of them. At first they were mostly factory made, so that I did not notice them, any more than I noticed the boards with warnings, except just to observe they were there. But coming among the Christs carved in wood by the peasant artists, I began to feel them. Now, it seems to me, they create almost an atmosphere over the northern Tirol, an atmosphere of pain.

I was going along a marshy place at the foot of the mountains, at evening, when the sky was a pale, dead colour and the hills were nearly black. At a meeting of the paths was a crucifix, and between the feet of the Christ a little red patch of dead poppies. So I looked at him. It was an old shrine, and the Christus was nearly like a man. He seemed to me to be real. In front of me hung a Bavarian peasant, a Christus, staring across at the evening and the black hills. He had broad cheek-bones and sturdy limbs, and he hung doggedly on the cross, hating it. He reminded me of a peasant farmer, fighting slowly and meanly, but not giving in. His plain, rudimentary face stared stubbornly at the hills, and his neck was stiffened, as if even yet he were struggling away from the cross he resented. He would not yield to it. I stood in front of him, and realized him. He might have said, "Yes, here I am, and it's bad enough, and it's suffering, and it doesn't come to an end. *Perhaps* something will happen, will help. If it doesn't, I s'll have to go on with it." He seemed stubborn and struggling from the root of his soul, his human soul. No God-ship had been thrust upon him. He was human clay, a peasant Prometheus-Christ, his poor soul bound in him, blind, but struggling stubbornly against the fact of the nails. And I looked across at the tiny square of orange light, the window of a farmhouse on the marsh. And, thinking of the other little farms, of how the man and his wife and his children worked on till dark, intent and silent, carrying the hay in their arms out of the streaming thunder-rain which soaked them through, I understood how the Christus was made.

And after him, when I saw the Christs posing on the Cross, à la Guido Reni,[3] I recognized them as the mere conventional symbol,

---

[3] Guido Reni (1575-1642), an Italian painter whose work was characterized often by insipid sentiment and a lack of vitality.

meaning no more Christ than St. George and the Dragon on a five-shilling-piece means England.

There are so many Christs carved by men who have carved to get at the meaning of their own soul's anguish. Often, I can distinguish one man's work in a district. In the Zemm valley, right in the middle of the Tirol, there are some half-dozen crucifixes by the same worker, who has whittled away in torment to see himself emerge out of the piece of timber, so that he can understand his own suffering, and see it take on itself the distinctness of an eternal thing, so that he can go on further, leaving it. The chief of these crucifixes is a very large one, deep in the Klamm, where it is always gloomy and damp. The river roars below, the rock wall opposite reaches high overhead, pushing back the sky. And by the track where the pack-horses go, in the cold gloom, hangs the large, pale Christ. He has fallen forward, just dead, and the weight of his full-grown, mature body is on the nails of the hands. So he drops, as if his hands would tear away, and he would fall to earth. The face is strangely brutal, and is set with an ache of weariness and pain and bitterness, and his rather ugly, passionate mouth is shut with bitter despair. After all, he had wanted to live and to enjoy his manhood. But fools had ruined his body, and thrown his life away, when he wanted it. No one had helped. His youth and health and vigour, all his life, and himself, were just thrown away as waste. He had died in bitterness. It is sombre and damp, silent save for the roar of water. There hangs the falling body of the man who had died in bitterness of spirit, and the driver of the pack-horses takes off his hat, cringing in his sturdy cheerfulness as he goes beneath.

He is afraid. I think of the carver of the crucifix. He also was more or less afraid. They all, when they carved or erected these crucifixes, had fear at the bottom of their hearts. And so the monuments to physical pain are found everywhere in the mountain gloom. By the same hand that carved the big, pale Christ I found another crucifix, a little one, at the end of a bridge. This Christ had a fair beard instead of a black one, and his body was hanging differently. But there was about him the same bitterness, the same despair, even a touch of cynicism. Evidently the artist could not get beyond the tragedy that tormented him. No wonder the peasants are afraid, as they take off their hats in passing up the valley.

They are afraid of physical pain. It terrifies them. Then they raise, in their startled helplessness of suffering, these Christs, these human attempts at deciphering the riddle of pain. In the same way they paint the humorous little pictures of some calamity—a man drowned in a stream or killed by a falling tree—and nail it up near the scene of the accident. "Memento mori," they say everywhere. And so they try to get used to the idea of death and suffering, to rid themselves of some of the fear thereof. And all tragic art is part of the same attempt.

But some of the Christs are quaint. One I know is very elegant, brushed and combed. "I'm glad I am no lady," I say to him. For he is a pure lady-killer. But he ignores me utterly, the exquisite. The man who made him must have been dying to become a gentleman.

And a fair number are miserable fellows. They put up their eyebrows plaintively, and pull down the corners of their mouths. Sometimes they gaze heavenwards. They are quite sorry for themselves.

"Never mind," I say to them. "It'll be worse yet, before you've done."

Some of them look pale and done-for. They didn't make much fight; they hadn't much pluck in them. They make me sorry.

"It's a pity you hadn't got a bit more kick in you," I say to them. And I wonder why in England one sees always this pale, pitiful Christ with no "go" in him. Is it because our national brutality is so strong and deep that we must create for ourselves an anaemic Christus, for ever on the whine; either that, or one of those strange neutrals with long hair, that are supposed to represent to our children the Jesus of the New Testament.

In a tiny glass case beside the high-road where the Isar is a very small stream, sits another Christ that makes me want to laugh, and makes me want to weep also. His little head rests on his hand, his elbow on his knee, and he meditates, half-wearily. I am strongly reminded of Walther von der Vogelweide [4] and the German medieval spirit. Detached, he sits, and dreams, and broods, in his little golden crown of thorns, and his little cloak of red flannel, that some peasant woman has stitched for him.

---

[4] Walther von der Vogelweide (1170-1230), the leading poet and minnesinger of medieval Germany, was born near Sterzing.

"*Couvre-toi de gloire, Tartarin—couvre-toi de flanelle,*" [5] I think to myself.

But he sits, a queer little man, fretted, plunged in anxiety of thought, and yet dreaming rather pleasantly at the same time. I think he is the forefather of the warm-hearted German philosopher and professor.

He is the last of the remarkable Christs of the peasants that I have seen. Beyond the Brenner an element of unreality seems to creep in. The Christs are given great gashes in the breast and knees, and from the brow and breast and hands and knees streams of blood trickle down, so that one sees a weird striped thing in red and white that is not at all a Christus. And the same red that is used for the blood serves also to mark the path, so that one comes to associate the *Martertafeln* and their mess of red stripes with the stones smeared with scarlet paint for guidance. The wayside chapels, going south, become fearfully florid and ornate, though still one finds in them the little wooden limbs, arms and legs and feet, and little wooden cows or horses, hung up by the altar, to signify a cure in these parts. But there is a tendency for the Christs themselves to become either neuter or else sensational. In a chapel near St. Jakob, a long way from the railway, sat the most ghastly Christus I can imagine. He is seated, after the crucifixion. His eyes, which are turned slightly to look at you, are bloodshot till they glisten scarlet, and even the iris seems purpled. And the misery, the almost criminal look of hate and misery on the bloody, disfigured face is shocking. I was amazed at the ghastly thing: moreover, it was fairly new.

South of the Brenner again, in the Austrian Tirol, I have not seen anyone salute the Christus: not even the guides. As one goes higher the crucifixes get smaller and smaller. The wind blows the snow under the tiny shed of a tiny Christ: the guides tramp stolidly by, ignoring the holy thing. That surprised me. But perhaps these were particularly unholy men. One does not expect a great deal of an Austrian, except real pleasantness.

So, in Austria, I have seen a fallen Christus. It was on the

---

[5] "Cover thyself with glory, Tartarin—cover thyself with flannel," two injunctions addressed (in Chapter VI) to the comic hero of the nineteenth-century French novel, *Tartarin de Tarascon* by Alphonse Daudet, in order to suggest the dual nature of man: the aspiring, heroic soul and the reluctant, earthbound body.

Jaufen, not very far from Meran. I was looking at all the snowpeaks all around, and hurrying downhill, trying to get out of a piercing wind, when I almost ran into a very old *Martertafel*. The wooden shed was silver-grey with age, and covered on the top with a thicket of lichen, weird, grey-green, sticking up its tufts. But on the rocks at the foot of the cross was the armless Christ, who had tumbled down and lay on his back in a weird attitude. It was one of the old, peasant Christs, carved out of wood, and having the long, wedge-shaped shins and thin legs that are almost characteristic. Considering the great sturdiness of a mountaineer's calves, these thin, flat legs are interesting. The arms of the fallen Christ had broken off at the shoulders, and they hung on their nails, as ex *voto* [6] limbs hang in the shrines. But these arms dangled from their palms, one at each end of the cross, the muscles, carved in wood, looking startling, upside down. And the icy wind blew them backwards and forwards. There, in that bleak place among the stones, they looked horrible. Yet I dared not touch either them or the fallen image. I wish some priest would go along and take the broken thing away.

So many Christs there seem to be: one in rebellion against his cross, to which he was nailed; one bitter with the agony of knowing he must die, his heart-beatings all futile; one who felt sentimental; one who gave in to his misery; one who was a sensationalist; one who dreamed and fretted with thought. Perhaps the peasant carvers of crucifixes are right, and all these were found on the same cross. And perhaps there were others too: one who waited for the end, his soul still with a sense of right and hope; one ashamed to see the crowd make beasts of themselves, ashamed that he should provide for their sport; one who looked at them and thought: "And I am of you. I might be among you, yelling at myself in that way. But I am not, I am here. And so——"

All those Christs, like a populace, hang in the mountains under their little sheds. And perhaps they are falling, one by one. And I suppose we have carved no Christs, afraid lest they should be too like men, too like ourselves. What we worship must have exotic form.

---

[6] Votive.

# OUTSIDE LITERATURE

## *Joseph Conrad*

Joseph Conrad (1857-1924), born and educated in Poland, entered upon a career in the French and English merchant marine in 1873. He gave up the sea in the 1890's, when, having taught himself English by reading a newspaper, he embarked on a new career as a writer of English novels. Most of his novels have nautical backgrounds, and all are written in a luxuriant style highly sensitive to subtleties of character and atmosphere. In this essay he considers the merits of a prose style much different from his own, that of "Notices to Mariners," a periodic publication of the British Admiralty which gives essential information on ship channels, ocean currents, and navigational aids.

This essay appeared originally in the Manchester Guardian (December 4, 1922) and is reprinted from Last Essays (1926).

Having been prompted by a certain literary suggestion to reflect upon the nature of Notices to Mariners, I fell to examining some of my old feelings and impressions which, strictly professional as they were, have yet contributed in the end toward the existence of a certain amount of literature; or, at any rate, of pages of prose. The Notices to Mariners are good prose, but I think no critic would admit them into the body of literature. And it is only as compositions in prose that I believe myself competent to speak of them. And, first, let me thank God that they do not belong to imaginative literature. It would be dreadful if they did. An imaginatively-written Notice to Mariners would be a deadly thing. I mean it literally. It would be sure to kill a number of people before its imaginative quality had been appreciated and suppressed. That their style must be clear and concise, and the punctuation of the ordinary kind, would not necessarily militate against their being regarded as literature. The maxims

11

of La Rochefoucauld[1] are concise enough. But they open horizons; they plumb the depths; they make us squirm, shudder, smile in turn; and even sigh—at times; whereas the prose of the Notices to Mariners must do nothing of the kind.

And it doesn't. A mariner detected shuddering or sighing over a Notice to Mariners would simply (to speak in unliterary language) be not fit for his job. All means of acting on man's spiritual side are forbidden to that prose. In those compositions which are read as earnestly as anything that ever came from printing press, all suggestion of Love, of Adventure, of Romance, of Speculation, of all that decorates and ennobles life, except Responsibility, is barred. What we expect from them is not suggestion but information of an ideal accuracy, such as you do not find in the prose of the works on science, which is mainly imaginative and often solemnly mystifying. That is why some quite decent men are moved to smile as they read it. But there is no mystification in the language of truth contained in the Notices to Mariners. You would not want to smile at them. No decent man would. Even Mr. Punch,[2] to whom as a great burlesque poet nothing is supposed to be sacred, and who has been seen lately taking liberties with the explosive atom, would not dream of making fun out of Notices to Mariners. Mr. Punch knows better. He knows that for an inspired poet who sees the mystic relations of sublunary matters, Notices to Mariners are things to be read reverently. They are like declarations of a minutely careful Providence. They can be imagined as dictated in a quiet voice by the angel who, in the words of the song, sits aloft to watch over poor Jack. They belong to a prose which, if certainly not immortal, is revelatory to its own generation.

Addressed to a special public, limited to a very definite special subject, having no connection with the intellectual culture of mankind, and yet of some importance to a civilisation which is founded on the protection of life and property, that prose has only one ideal to attain, to hold on to: the ideal of perfect accuracy. You would

---

[1] François de La Rochefoucauld (1613-1680), French author whose epigrammatic maxims, published as *Réflexions ou sentences et maximes morales* (1665), are examples of a precise and lucid prose style.

[2] "Mr. Punch" is the name given collectively to the contributors to the popular British magazine of wit and humor, *Punch*.

say that such an ideal may easily be captured by a steady, prosaic mind devoting itself for a few minutes (the Notices to Mariners are short) every day to the task of composition. Why, yes! But what about misprints—the bane of authors?

And then the absences. I mean the absences of mind. It is a fact that the most pedestrian mind will sometimes take a flight from the office where it works (I suppose Notices to Mariners are written in some sort of office) toward subjects of poetic fancy, its children, its lady-love, its glass of beer, and such other things interesting to its mortal envelope. I often wondered what the author of Notices to Mariners looks like. I have tried to represent him to myself as a monk, a man who has renounced the vanities of the world, and for preference belonging to the Order of Trappists who are bidden to remember death—*memento mori*—and nothing else. A sobering thought! Just suppose the author of Notices to Mariners acquiring convivial habits and sitting down to write a Notice in that happy frame of mind when nothing matters much and one letter of the alphabet is as good as another. For myself—who am not convivial in that sense and have written a varied lot of prose with a quite ridiculous scrupulosity and an absurd seriousness—I don't mind confessing that if I were told to write a Notice to Mariners I would not pray perhaps—for I have my own convictions about the abuse of prayer—but I would certainly fast. I would fast in the evening and get up to write my Notice to Mariners at four o'clock in the morning for fear of accidents. One letter is so soon written for another—with fatal results.

It happened to me many years ago to endanger the course of my humble career at sea simply by writing the letter W instead of the letter E at the bottom of a page full of figures. It was an examination and I ought to have been plucked mercilessly. But in consideration, I believe, of all my other answers being correct, I was handed that azimuth paper back by the examiner's assistant, with the calm remark, "You have fourteen minutes yet." I looked at the face of the clock; it was round like the moon, white as a ghost, unfeeling, idiotic. I sat down under it with the conviction of the crushing materiality of time, and calling in my mind the assistant examiner a sarcastic brute. For no man could have gone over all those figures in fourteen minutes. I hope my exasperated consternation at this check could not be detected. It was funny even to myself. Then, just at the moment when my sinking heart had touched bottom, I saw the error staring at me, enormous, gross, palpable. I traced hastily a capital E over the W, and went back to the desk with my sheet of blue paper in a still shaky hand. The assistant hardly glanced at it before he let it drop, and I saw then that in my lack of comprehension it was I who had been an unqualified brute. For in his remark about the fourteen minutes he had clearly tried to give me a hint. He was a charming young man, obviously poor, with an intelligent, as if suffering, face. Not exactly sickly but delicate. A sea voyage would have done him good. But it was I who went to sea—this time bound to Calcutta.

And it was in Calcutta, a few months afterwards, that one morning my captain on going ashore saw me busy about the decks and beckoned to me in that way ship-masters have, or used to have. I mean ship-masters who commanded their ships from truck to keelson as it were, technically and spiritually, in motion and at rest, and through every moment of their life, when the seaman's calling was by the mere force of its conditions more vocational than it can be at the present day. My ship-master had that way of beckoning. What way? Well—all I can say of it is that one dropped everything. I can't describe it better. So I dropped whatever I was doing and he said: "You will find a Notice on the cabin table. Go in and enter it on the proper Admiralty sheet. Do it now." Which I hastened to do.

That examination, the issue of which had hung on a capital letter, had caused me to be officially certified as fit to undertake that particular duty; and ever since then my familiarity with Notices to Mariners, which are not literature, went on growing through a course of years, up to the moment when stepping ashore for the last time I lost all touch with the most trusted kind of printed prose. Henceforth I had to begin (while totally unprovided with Notices to Authors) to write prose myself; and the pains I took with it only my Maker knows! And yet I never learned to trust it. I can't trust it to this day. We who write prose which is not that of the Notices to Mariners are forgotten by Providence. No angel watches us at our toil. A dreadful doubt hangs over the whole achievement of literature; I mean that of its greatest and its humblest men. Wasn't it

"Papa Augier" [3] who, being given a copy of *Hamlet*, glanced through it expertly and then dropped it with the dry remark: "*Vous appelez ça une pièce, vous?*" The whole tragedy of art lies in the nut-shell of this terrifying anecdote. But it never will occur to anybody to question the prosaic force of the author of Notices to Mariners, which are not literature, and his fidelity to his honourable ideal— the ideal of perfect accuracy.

---

[3] Emile Augier (1820-1889), French dramatist, whose comment on Shakespeare's *Hamlet*—"You call *that* a play?"—reflects his disapproval of its rambling structure and its lack of didactic bourgeois morality.

# A LOST WOOD

## H. M. Tomlinson

H. M. Tomlinson (1873-1958), born in the East End of
London, had little formal education, but he read intensively
in the work of such authors as Emerson, Whitman, and
Melville. These helped form his literary tastes and also gave
support to ideals of independence and simplicity that find
little comfort in modern progress. The author of novels and
many essays, he also wrote what is now a classic in travel
literature, The Sea and the Jungle (1912).

This essay was written in 1925 and is reprinted from
Out of Soundings (1931).

A critic of letters was discussing the French Romantics, and he dismissed, with but an impatient glance at it, a suggestion by one of us
that Rousseau was a harbinger of the Revolution.[1] Literature, so the
critic said, could do less to cause a general uproar than dear bread.
Books, one gathered from the critic, and he knew more of them than
did we who listened, were quite unrelated to the emotions of the
multitude, which discharged in thunder and lightning provoked no
more by poetry than by daisy-chains.

The critic may have been right. I expect the change in us
wrought by poetry is so slow in the showing that when the trans-
mutation is complete we know of no change. We cannot see what
has happened to us. The poet, having done in his brief life his best,
may get what comfort he can out of that. We are certainly obstinate
in our old ways, conservative with flint arrowheads or any other
familiar notion, and unmoved by revolutions which come about in
imperceptible degrees. And could Sinai itself impose its revelation
on a climber who was no Moses? All most of us would discern at

---

[1] Jean Jacques Rousseau (1712-1778), French philosopher, novelist, and social
theorist, whose criticism of absolute monarchy as cruel, oppressive, and contrary
to the laws of nature was seized upon during the French Revolution and used
as partial justification of the outbreaks against the government.

the summit of Sinai would be the uncomfortable draught sweeping the barren rocks.

It is probable, we are forced to confess, that a few years of petrol have made a greater difference in the world of men than all the poets since Homer. To judge by the reformed highways and byways of England, and the talk of our neighbours, petrol has moved us more than all our converse with great literature. Petrol is more popular than religion, and whirls to delight a vast multitude of people who would remain as unaffected by Bach as a congregation of penguins. If the test were made, perhaps a little argument directed towards the choice of the right sort of motor-car might more easily raise a group of people to eloquence, than an insult to the Trinity. Petrol is even dissolving the face of the English landscape. We are exchanging our woodlands for tarmac, and although tarmac is known to be kind to rubber tyres, yet its tolerance is hardly sufficient to compensate for the loss of swathes of orchards, meadows, and ancient buildings. One does not complain about this, for it would be just as foolish to complain of the untimeliness of a phase of the moon.

Yet regret and disquietude, despite the improvements we are making in our condition, remain with us, for we cannot forget our poets, and what once inspired them to sing to us. Once there was a scrap of Surrey, which I had grown to accept as casually as one does those things whose importance is known when they are gone. I think it was only common English countryside. There was nothing in it that a building contractor should desire it. Nobody with an eye to the future saw anything there. Its gravel soil was not worth an advertisement. But it had a desultory lane, with walnut, lime and beech trees, and on a morning in late summer you were not likely to meet anything in it but a farm waggon laden with dried peppermint; mint and lavender were cultivated locally, and our only factories had stills for the extraction of essences from herbs. The smell in the wake of that waggon on a hot day was a surprising suggestion of the virtue of Surrey earth.

I could not say the war began to change it, but it seems so. I do know that one part of the land, and corn grew there, through which the lane meandered, became very swiftly an aerodrome; and the aerodrome has not yet convinced me that it is better to see flying machines at their graceful evolutions than a field of wheat with a

little wind and much sun on it. Alas, we were too busy then to
consider in calmness the nature of the changes we were bringing
about. I remember that, in the years of long ago, before we were
even educated as far as the signs of Zeppelins by night, we had
neighbouring ponds fed by springs in the chalk. At the bottom of
one deep, transparent pool you could see a spring uprising; shadows
coiled in the beryl. That was where, within twelve miles of Charing
Cross, we watched a pair of kingfishers feeding their six youngsters;
the babies sat in a row on an osier twig, which was oblique with their
weight. The darting blue and chestnut of those neighbours of ours
greatly distinguished us. One lucky young friend of mine saw in the
same secluded grove, and as late as the days of the air-raids, a golden
oriole. He still remembers it. To hear him talk of that wonderful
visitor you might suppose that one day on his way home from school,
where he had been learning of the brave things that were, he had
surprised a dryad, who slipped into the bushes, but not before he
could name her. Does Apollo live? So much was possible to him,
that day.

Does he live? Well, not there; not now. Petrol has acted like
magic on the place. Miraculous stuff, petrol! But the kingfishers do
not like it. Nor does the lane wander any more. It has been disciplined, and we know how good is discipline. The lane is broad, it is
direct. It has no dust, and has lost its smell of herbs. The old walnut
trees do not lean over broken pales there. There are no trees. The
lane has become a straight road with a surface like polished ebony.
It is, in fact, a highway for motor-cars. It becomes dangerous, every
Sunday morning, with an endless flying procession of engines on
their way to the coast; the chain reverses towards evening. We do
not hear the corncrake any more, when coolness and silence fall at
eventide; we hear klaxons.[2] We have no peppermint fields; we have
filling stations. Our springs and ponds, owing to an increase in the
value of gravel sites, have lapsed into areas of mud which cannot
determine to dry completely, and are desolate with discarded tins.
As for the golden oriole, you might as well look for a seraph. Petrol
has achieved all that. We do not say a word against it, but merely
point to the fact. It would be just as useful to interrupt, as a protest,

---

[2] Electric horns once widely used on automobiles; the name was originally a
trade-mark.

the line of cars flying to the coast on a Sunday, in a moment of desperation and anger. There the cars are; they move faster than peppermint waggons, and modern youth often steers them in a fashion that mocks mortality.

It is easy to understand the popularity of petrol. As a stimulant, it is taking the place of beer and whisky. Rousseau may not have helped to cause a revolution, but there is no doubt about the common emotion which petrol evokes. Petrol is taken, not in the hope that it will transport us to any better place, but merely that it will remove us swiftly from where we are. It is the latest anodyne in these years of discontent and irresolution. It would be ridiculous to expect us to know what we ought to do, for we do not always know what we want to do. Petrol settles the difficulty. We get into a car, and start the explosions within its powerful engine; then we are compelled to do something. We join an endless line of headlong vehicles, and to continue to be irresolute would be perilous. Last summer I trudged over a road, once a by-path in the West of England which a tramp could have for himself for most of a long day. I hoped there to meet a ghost or two from the past, because they used to know that road very well; and they might turn up, if the news got to them that I was there again. But I did not meet them. I met instead a procession of astonishing charabancs, some from Manchester, others from Birmingham, and one from as far as Glasgow. There was no room for a pedestrian but in the drains by the roadside, where he had to stride for safety through soiled nettles and briars. The local inns were no longer places of refreshment and gossip. About one of those inns, and I had had my mind set on it for an hour, a dozen huge social cars were parked. The road was bright with pools of black grease. The orchard of the inn was sad, through traffic for which orchards are not grown. And no room could be had at the bar, nor elsewhere within, for an idle traveller who had time to waste; other travellers were there, continually arriving and departing. They had no time to waste. Yet these travellers of the new kind appeared to be satisfied merely with travelling. They knew not why they were there; they had paid their fares. They stood about, waiting for the signal that they were to be whirled on again, with their backs to a land which is as good as most in Europe. They did not look at it. It did not exist in its reality for them; it was only on their route. They were satisfied with the knowledge that they were there; they could prove it with picture-postcards which could be bought at the inn counter.

Very early one morning, when on a voyage from the East, I was startled from sleep by a seaman. He had switched on my cabin light; it was summer, but he stood there chilling the cabin with his wet overcoat. What was wrong?

"Nothing, sir; the chief officer wants you on the bridge."

I went up hurriedly, in pyjamas and oil-skins. Day had not come, but it was not night; night was lifted slightly in the east on a wedge of rose, though the wind was still bleak out of darkness. We were somewhere near the Berlengas.[3] What was this? My friend the chief officer pointed astern without a word. We were passing a ghost ship, under all canvas. The barque was so close that I could see the length of her deck. She was silent, and more pale than the twilight. She was tall, and tinctured faintly with rose. Had we steamed back into another age? Was the past so near? I could see two men on her poop, but they were not looking at us. Only my friend, and the bridge of our liner, were material. My friend spoke. "I thought you would like to see her; it may be the last time. Isn't she a beauty?"

Even with my eye still on the receding barque I felt that sailor's behaviour was more curious than what he had wakened me to watch. His jacket, I had noticed, bore a row and a half of decorations won in war; he was a hard and busy officer; he infested that great liner like a stern challenge whose whereabouts was uncertain until he strode round a corner, and then he never stopped unless there was something which must be said. This unexpected tenderness of his for what was hardly more than a gracious apparition in a delusive hour surprised me; yet he had been so sure, without reason, that I, too, would have the eye to see the spectre, that he had summoned me from bed into the hour when there is no courage. We stood talking up aloft till the sun came and saw us.

So, though I dare not deny the critic who mocked the power of poetry to work upon us to as good a purpose as starvation, yet perhaps he was too trifling with the spell of what is imponderable. Our

---

[3] The Berlengas are a group of small islands in the Atlantic off Portugal.

mutability, like the wind which bloweth where it listeth, is subject to
sorceries having the necessity of the very laws which send zephyrs or
hurricanes out of the immane.[4] How often has a fond memory or
sentiment, so doubtfully valid in garish daylight that we would not
show it to a friend, decided us to an enterprise? And we were right.
For that reason, the older we get, the more we doubt the obvious
clue to any story; we have found too often that what was unrevealed
at the time was more potent than anything we heard when the knowing people were explaining it. But for a barque appearing near us
one morning, I should have thought my friend the chief officer was
no more open to zephyrs and faint hints than the steel under us.
That steel was obvious and compelling, and he was part of it. And
after that voyage he sent a letter to me, disclosing a burden which
not for a moment did I suspect a modern liner to carry. He was glad,
he explained, to get out of London again. He called his steamer's
bridge, which to me seemed to govern affairs large and complex
enough to require a borough council for their management, his
sanctuary. He showed a revulsion from our city which was as spon-
taneous and unreasonable as would be a mahatma's from a riot. He
said his bridge, in the morning watch, was the only place where he
could meet himself. He warned me that in London I should never
meet myself. London frightened him. London was on no course.
London was adrift. Its size and unrest were so like delirium that he
ran from it. "Those new buildings you've got, they're Egyptian, I
tell you, they're horrible. Something has gone wrong with you if you
like them. You'd better look out. They squat on the mind, ugly
square masses, like tombs. I don't want to be under them, as
though I had no name, drifting at the bottom of them with the
drainage of life which doesn't know where it is going. It doesn't,
does it?" He said he only found himself again when watching his
ship's head grow bright in the dawn, and nothing around but the
empty sea, and the sun. Then he knew his name belonged to him,
and what he was doing, and why he was doing it, to some extent.

Perhaps rebellion comes as much as anything from the sense
that, as mere items in the paraphernalia of the State, we are losing
our identity. A slave may have a soul, and possess it in patience, but

---

[4] Vast.

not an automaton. Made homogeneous by machinery, we have but one name now; we are the nation. And when our governing machines, multiplying and expanding, claiming greater space for their wheels, flatten and unify still more the ancient, varied, and familiar things which we did not know were good till they had gone, we feel as though our identity will soon be traceless. We become a little fearful and desperate. It is as though a chilling air were felt from unseen ice gradually advancing, warning of another glacial age, to put our name and works with the Neanderthalers. We rebel from the suggestion that we must go under the cold mass of a mindless necessity.

It was April; and that was a disturbing letter to receive when the primroses were due. I had no chance to reassure myself of my name by watching a ship's head grow bright in a broad dawn. Egypt for me and the necessary rod! [5] All I could do was to rebel for a day. I would decline to make a single brick. I began to walk away from the arid masses of London's honey-combed limestone, monuments of servitude, though was careful to begin my escape at the ten-mile radius.[6] I remembered that it was some years since I had walked in that direction, for the paths I used to know appeared to have been mislaid. Escape was not so easy from new, wide, straight and asphalted thoroughfares dangerous with swift engines. Aeroplanes were chanting overhead, but no larks. A raw inflammation of villas was spreading through a valley, which was green when last I saw it. Then my companion, he who once met a golden oriole, remembered a little wood in a hollow, aside from the traffic. That, he told me, would certainly be there. Nobody would have interfered with that. He found the lane to it, after some bewilderment with his bearings, which had shifted somewhat. There was no doubt that this was the lane, he declared at last, but dubiously. It was? Then we must suffer it, erupted and raw. Its hedges, bearing the first leaves of the year, were displaced, and their roots were higher than their boughs. In some lengths of the lane granite kerbs had replaced the hedges, and an iron sink-hole or two improved the ditches. A new path, a motor-

---

[5] Possibly a reference to Egypt as the task that Moses could not set aside (Exodus 4) and to the rod as the scourge of God (as in Job 9:34 and 21:9).

[6] A zone with a ten-mile radius, measured from Charing Cross as the center, beyond which an additional surcharge on taxi fare is applied.

lorry careened midway in its deep mud, went directly into the wood. On the verge of the wood the hazels had been crushed and splintered, and their golden tassels hung disconsolate, as though we were on the track of a recent and lusty mastodon.

Improvement had come. In the heart of the wood, oaks were being felled, and by the torn roots of one was a dead hedgehog, which had been evicted from its hybernaculum[7] into the frigid blast of reform. Unseen near to us a saw was at work, and its voice was like the incessant growling of a carnivore which had got its teeth into a body and would never let go. This Easter, by all the signs, was the last the wood would see. The bluebells had been coming, expecting no evil, and, had they been allowed the grace of a few more weeks, they would have put the depth of the sky between the trees; but carts and engines had crushed them, and had even exposed their white bulbs, as though the marrow of the wood were exposed.

I do not say the Easter message of that wood was especially deplorable. I knew it was possible and even right to see those granite kerbs and the cleared foundations as an urgent message of life and growth. The children of men would play in new gardens there, in another Easter. Still, somehow that direct and unquestioning attack by our machines, especially on the fragile windflowers, was more dismaying than inclement weather. A mastodon might really have been there, with no mind but in its tusks, irresistible and forthright. "I thought you would like to see her; it may be the last time. Isn't she a beauty?" It may be that the sense of beauty has no survival value, to use a term of our biological appraisers; nevertheless, it does survive, so we may suppose there is something as primordial in it as in acquisitiveness. When we see the defacement of beauty we continue to feel as though light were put out in ignorance. And what we want, as certainly as new villas, is more light. Is there a light to check us when we are steering our wheels over the windflowers, the Pasque blossoms, and are replacing them with stones?

There were Greek pagans long ago, and some of their work clearly had a value by which, though not useful, it has survived; and the idle fancy was theirs that the windflower was stained with the blood of Adonis, slain by a boar, and that its pallor was from the

---

[7] Winter quarters of a hibernating animal.

tears of Aphrodite, who sorrowed over the beautiful youth. Even our own pagans, before Augustine gave their thoughts another direction, felt bound to conclude that the windflower was painted by the elves. Who else could have veined so delicately that fabric? Who else would have inspired daintiness with that modesty in the half-light of the woods?

Behind me I heard the motor-lorry heaving itself out of the mire it had made. It backed and crashed like a hippopotamus into another tracery of mist and emerald, and Adonis died again. I buttoned up my coat against the northerly blast. Let Adonis die. We cannot help him. The tears of Aphrodite are of no avail against the tusks of boars. Only the bolts of Zeus could prevail against the progress of our engines; and Olympus, we have been most credibly informed for many Easters past, is "to let"; and if we must believe the reports of our busy agents of estates, then it is about the only place that is to let.

Yet one of the things I clearly remember of the war was a blue-bell. It was in Thiepval wood.[8] Men who have reason to keep in mind the valley of the Ancre will smile at that. Thiepval had come to its end. Our engines had been there, had gone over it, and were loudly progressing elsewhere on the eastern hills. It was April, but there was no wood, no village, and no old château, though a little down the slope towards St. Pierre Divion was a tank on its side; one of the automata, too, had died. Life had gone; nothing was there but mud, bones, rags, helmets, broken rifles, and skulls. Thiepval was Golgotha. We were turning from it, but were stopped by a fleck of colour in the drab wreckage; life had already returned to Thiepval? It was a wild hyacinth. One bluebell to all April! What, still there and unafraid?

One may dare to hope that the marrow of earth has a more stubborn vitality than our dismay allowed; it may survive our engines? It survived the glaciers. After all, there may be in the frail wind-flower a virtue that will outlast the lorries. We have been surprised, before this, by the shy patience of what may have been lovely and of good report, yet otherwise was inexcusable. The slight but haughty

---

[8] The scene of heavy fighting in the battle of the Somme in World War I; St.-Pierre-de-Divion is a small twelfth-century church a few miles northwest of Thiepval on the left bank of the Ancre.

gesture of my sailor friend, one dawn, saluting from the bridge of his ship the beauty of the world, no more valuable though it was than the pagan thought which celebrated Adonis in the petals of the windflower, may have been a sign that nothing could deflect a barque he knew from her right course. And how else could he prove his faith? He summoned me as a witness, he was so sure of fellowship. Yet there is no mathematics to support him.

# A SENTIMENTAL JOURNEY

## Ivor Brown

Ivor Brown, born in 1891 in Penang, Malaya, of Scottish parentage and educated at Oxford, is a novelist, journalist, linguist, and essayist. He has written for the Manchester Guardian, the London Saturday Review, and other papers. In a collection of essays about London (Winter in London, 1951), he comments: "A man is a fool who does not study and savour the place in which he lives."

This essay appeared originally in a short version in the Saturday Review (July 18, 1925) and is reprinted from Masques and Phases (1926).

A quarter of a century is a phrase with an epochal ring and these last five and twenty years have altered the world more than most. Empires have waxed and waned; motor-cars have altered the whole face of travel and the whole scale of British distances; a penny has become a halfpenny and the char-à-banc has crashed its way through the silent austerities of the Scottish Sabbath. But much of Scotland stands exactly where it did. Here in the north-east, whither I have made my sentimental journey, the land and sea yield the old harvests of grain and herring. The plough that has not altered since Homer told its shape and motion [1] is not to suffer change while a boy grows up. The sea shows more of steam and less of sail, but evolution has obliged Tennessee [2] by signally failing to leave new marks on herring and haddock, rabbit and hare. Had I been a London boy, I could hardly go in search of my youth. For the horses of the green Atlas bus that took me to Lord's have vanished and no more is the effort-

---

[1] In the Iliad, x. 353, and the Odyssey, xviii. 374.

[2] Tennessee statutes, having adopted the Fundamentalist belief in a single divine act of Creation as related in the Bible, stipulated that the theory of continuing evolution should not be taught in the public schools. At the time this essay was written, John Scopes had been brought to trial in Dayton for having violated the law.

less beauty of J. T. Hearne's bowling to be observed.[3] But here I can go to "the games" last visited in 1900 and they will be held in the same "haugh"; [4] the same dancing-master will sit on the judgment bench to nod gravely at the same flings and sword-dances. The pipes will be mournful and brisk with the same airs and tea-time will bring the same neat bag of cakes. True, the programme hinted at the presence of the Abertochty "jazz band." But what's in a name? As of old there were fiddlers three.

The conditions, as they say, are eminently suitable. Here one may indeed go in search of one's youth and reconstruct in the tranquillity of a sunny afternoon the emotions of a very small boy. Of course it is all much smaller than one's memory. A mile has dwindled to a furlong, a forest to a copse, a torrent to a trickle. The trout that were Tritons are now to be seen as flickering minnows in the shallows under the bridge. A mountain has shrunk to a hillock. It doesn't do, this retracing of boyhood's steps. One knew, of course, that looking backward is like looking through an opera-glass reversed. But the distortion is worse than one imagined. One shouldn't have gone. The return has been a cowardly assault upon romance, a butchering of innocent memories. Far better have left the old house to be, in mind's eye, grandiose, mysterious, abounding in dark possibilities; in short, the half-menacing, half-entrancing monster that it used to be. Far better have left to the gardens their flattering spaciousness of boyhood's vision, to the wood its pristine mystery of cavernous and black allure.

But one has done the deed. There it all lies, plain-set in smiling sunlight, a diminished paradise. It is just a piece of eastern Scotland, that frank and self-explanatory countryside which rolls an open bosom to the plain straightforward sea. No Celtic twilights, tortuous lochs, and peaks that stab the mist are here to make adult reason concede a tremor to romance. Good farming trims the landscape; grey, orderly walls keep watch over pasture, roots, and oats. Here and there the rising ground soars out of man's control and green fields admit their

---

[3] Lord's is the name of a cricket field in London where important matches are played. J. T. Hearne (1867-1944) has been described as the "nearest approach to perfection in a medium-paced, right-handed bowler that cricket has yet known." His great records were made before 1900.

[4] An alluvial field in a river valley (Scottish).

limitations and march peaceably with heather. Here the hillside turns to fir plantation, there to empty purple acres. But the wildness, the strangeness, the beckoning immensities of those old days have shrivelled and departed. Boyhood was too small for Ordnance maps and the withering accuracies of the measuring-rod. It made its own mileage, forged its own contours, made and named and ruled its mountain range. Compute it now coldly at "one inch to mile" and a kingdom turns to a crofter's holding. Yet within this nutshell moved a king of infinite space. Perhaps not king; a princeling were more accurate.

The owls have gone from the quivering pinewood; no heron flaps its pondering course along the burn. The coneys we have always with us, and their tribe at least is slow to dwindle. The gamekeeper has gone from the lodge, and he who knew the haunts of beast and bird now peddles bull's-eyes [5] and half-pounds of tea. He is an injured man. Somebody started a war, and there has been no need for small estates since then. A nice range of red deer, grouse, and salmon will fetch a doubled price from merchant princes, for we are not all paupers at holiday-time. But the solid "mixed shooting" with nothing showy about it and a four-square chunk of masonry to maintain attracts no bidders now. The lawns grow weeds, and the gamekeeper digs potatoes until the shop bell rings, and then he must weigh out another quarter of sweeties. He knows it is all wrong, but he says very little. He never goes near the house from which he has been driven. For relaxation he has his parlour, and there he sits with all the immobility of the soil-bound peasant looking at nothing, unless it is the past. "You'll notice the sea has worked in a lot," he says. "It's beating the land by a yard a year. It'll tak' a' the links. There's changes everywhere."

Yet was this visitation altogether a blundering folly? Has the sentimental journey proved altogether a wanton outrage upon sentiment? No; it has its powers of reassurance, its compensations, and its fair suggestions. The woods have lost their wonder, and their darkness is a plain, unghosted thing. But beauty has crept in. Boyhood never saw that. Boyhood never knew the exquisite proportion of this countryside in which the elements of sea, moor, tilth, pasture, and copse have been dispensed as though by some inspired chemist

---

[5] Hard candies.

of landscape. The place does yield its reparations and pays them in the currency of the eye's delight. How fitly the house lifts up its native stone, grey, unassuming, comfortably set! How lightly the bridge jumps the burn and leads to the village and the mellow-gardened manse. The sense of a desert has departed and the sense of a civilization has come in. If one no longer looks for eagles in the skies or marauders in the glades, one can look for shapeliness in homes and handsomeness in everything. And it is a handsome country garnished by diligence and fruitful under discipline. The grey-beard who comes down from his farm to judge the piping and dancing at the village games will not whine to you about bad times. He has the measure of the soil and of his agrarian competitors; he has whipped his land into a clean prosperity, and his cattle are known and feared at the Royal Northern Show. His sons have gone to the university, but he is just a little doubtful about the teaching at the village academy. They want a better man, and, from the sound of his voice, they mean to get one. To judge the pibrochs is the limit of his surrender to Gaelic dreaming. His youngest boy is going to be as great a man of medicine as ever went south from Aberdeen. He goes on Sunday to the kirk, thinks little of the minister, and has no qualms.

It was once a land of giants, black-bearded men, who came up from the coastal fisheries and sometimes took a small boy in their boat to see the odd harvest of their nets. It was full of dark pools and distant heights, of birds and animals, of hopes and panics and surprises. It is not at all like that now. Boy Scouts encamp themselves where once was desolation. The burn trills equably through small and genial copses. The fields run up to the heather, and the heather, a mere mile of it, runs down again to the fields. But the view is gracious, and the air earns all the compliments that Shakespeare paid to the less deserving climate of sluggish Inverness.[6] The land breeds pensive but not ungenial men whose philosophy has hard, clear lines. Boyhood turned honest farms into its land of fancy free, made every trout a salmon, and every cushat a capercailzie; other years see other things. It is not all loss.

All that has gone is quantity. Quality remains. No glory, save that of stature, has departed. Rather has glory increased. To go in search of one's youth is to have done with the nonsense preached

---

[6] In *Macbeth*, I.vi.1-10. Macbeth's castle was at Inverness.

with a sublime eloquence by Wordsworth in his ode on the Intimations of Immortality. To grow up in body is to grow up in spirit. The eye develops with the frame, appreciation with the spread of limb. The shades of the prison house with which the poet threatened adolescence are indeed the fiction of brain-sickly brooding. Take the village. What was it to a boy but the goal of a morning journey? There were lessons waiting in the study at the manse; there was toffee at the village-shop. But now I can see that village and praise the wisdom that built it under the woods and above the burn, in as sweet a nook as Scotland can contain. I can praise the fitness of its shaping, and see that the houses of native stone have grown up like living things in perfect kinship with their landscape. The queer house that is half a fortress, the manse that is at once kindly and formal like a domesticated kirk, home of stern virtues and of gentle flowers and fruit, the twist and surge of the rambling street—all these were nothing then. They are much now. My boyhood, at least, had no vision splendid to surround its practical journeying. It thought of guns, fishing-rods, and sweetmeats. It breathed no larger air.

So there is good in growing up. The boy cannot see the wood for the trees, the burn for the lurking trout, the moor for the possible excitements of beast and bird. Now beauty comes in, life's compensation for adventure. The compensation outweighs the loss. The village takes its place in the scheme of things; it is the work of generations of living, labouring men. Its crannied walls have the flowers which you may search for the ultimate mysteries. But the walls need not drive you so far into the by-ways of reflection. They have their more obvious story and are the testament of the grey, orderly, but not ungenial culture of eastern Scotland. So, at the end of a sentimental journey, one may bask without regrets. Wonder has gone, but admiration remains. The meadow has lost its mystery but found its meaning, and takes its place in a scheme of things far beyond the scope and range of childish mind. The black wood that housed Jack Redskin no longer enfolds imaginary denizens. Does it matter? It is beautiful now as well as black. The house in which I gladly lived has become the house at which I gladly look. It is a generous exchange. It is indeed worth while to go in search of one's youth. That is dead and may not be discovered. But all the things that boyhood missed, how excellent they are!

# MY WOOD

## E. M. *Forster*

E. M. Forster was born in 1879 in England and educated
at Cambridge. *He established a reputation as a novelist with*
A Room with a View *(1908) and, after two visits to India,*
A Passage to India *(1924), the novel to which he refers in
this essay. Since 1924 he has confined his literary activity to
the writing of essays, radio lectures, biography, and criticism.*
*This essay appeared originally in 1926 and is reprinted
from* Abinger Harvest *(1936).*

A few years ago I wrote a book which dealt in part with the difficulties of the English in India. Feeling that they would have had no
difficulties in India themselves, the Americans read the book freely.
The more they read it the better it made them feel, and a cheque to
the author was the result. I bought a wood with the cheque. It is
not a large wood—it contains scarcely any trees, and it is intersected,
blast it, by a public footpath. Still, it is the first property that I have
owned, so it is right that other people should participate in my
shame, and should ask themselves, in accents that will vary in horror,
this very important question: What is the effect of property upon
the character? Don't let's touch economics; the effect of private
ownership upon the community as a whole is another question—a
more important question, perhaps, but another one. Let's keep to
psychology. If you own things, what's their effect on you? What's
the effect on me of my wood? → placement of stress imp.

In the first place, it makes me feel heavy. Property does have
this effect. Property produces men of weight, and it was a man of
weight who failed to get into the Kingdom of Heaven.[1] He was not
wicked, that unfortunate millionaire in the parable, he was only
stout; he stuck out in front, not to mention behind, and as he wedged
himself this way and that in the crystalline entrance and bruised his

---

[1] Matthew 19: 24.

well-fed flanks, he saw beneath him a comparatively slim camel passing through the eye of a needle and being woven into the robe of
God. The Gospels all through couple stoutness and slowness. They
point out what is perfectly obvious, yet seldom realized: that if you
have a lot of things you cannot move about a lot, that furniture
requires dusting, dusters require servants, servants require insurance
stamps, and the whole tangle of them makes you think twice before
you accept an invitation to dinner or go for a bathe in the Jordan.
Sometimes the Gospels proceed further and say with Tolstoy [2] that
property is sinful; they approach the difficult ground of asceticism
here, where I cannot follow them. But as to the immediate effects
of property on people, they just show straightforward logic. It produces men of weight. Men of weight cannot, by definition, move like
the lightning from the East unto the West,[3] and the ascent of a
fourteen-stone bishop into a pulpit is thus the exact antithesis of the
coming of the Son of Man. My wood makes me feel heavy.

In the second place, it makes me feel it ought to be larger.

The other day I heard a twig snap in it. I was annoyed at first,
for I thought that someone was blackberrying, and depreciating the
value of the undergrowth. On coming nearer, I saw it was not a man
who had trodden on the twig and snapped it, but a bird, and I felt
pleased. My bird. The bird was not equally pleased. Ignoring the
relation between us, it took fright as soon as it saw the shape of my
face, and flew straight over the boundary hedge into a field, the
property of Mrs. Henessy, where it sat down with a loud squawk. It
had become Mrs. Henessy's bird. Something seemed grossly amiss
here, something that would not have occurred had the wood been
larger. I could not afford to buy Mrs. Henessy out, I dared not
murder her, and limitations of this sort beset me on every side. Ahab [4]
did not want that vineyard—he only needed it to round off his property, preparatory to plotting a new curve—and all the land around
my wood has become necessary to me in order to round off the wood.
A boundary protects. But—poor little thing—the boundary ought in
its turn to be protected. Noises on the edge of it. Children throw

---

[2] Leo Nikolayevich Tolstoy (1828-1910), prominent Russian novelist and social
  philosopher. He regarded property as essentially wicked, the manifestation of
  avarice and a natural provocation to violence.

[3] Matthew 24: 27.

[4] 1 Kings 21.

stones. A little more, and then a little more, until we reach the sea. Happy Canute! Happier Alexander! [5] And after all, why should even the world be the limit of possession? A rocket containing a Union Jack will, it is hoped, be shortly fired at the moon. Mars. Sirius. Beyond which . . . But these immensities ended by saddening me. I could not suppose that my wood was the destined nucleus of universal dominion—it is so very small and contains no mineral wealth beyond the blackberries. Nor was I comforted when Mrs. Henessy's bird took alarm for the second time and flew clean away from us all, under the belief that it belonged to itself.

In the third place, property makes its owner feel that he ought to do something to it. Yet he isn't sure what. A restlessness comes over him, a vague sense that he has a personality to express—the same sense which, without any vagueness, leads the artist to an act of creation. Sometimes I think I will cut down such trees as remain in the wood, at other times I want to fill up the gaps between them with new trees. Both impulses are pretentious and empty. They are not honest movements towards money-making or beauty. They spring from a foolish desire to express myself and from an inability to enjoy what I have got. Creation, property, enjoyment form a sinister trinity in the human mind. Creation and enjoyment are both very, very good, yet they are often unattainable without a material basis, and at such moments property pushes itself in as a substitute, saying, "Accept me instead—I'm good enough for all three." It is not enough. It is, as Shakespeare said of lust, "The expense of spirit in a waste of shame": it is "Before, a joy proposed; behind, a dream." [6] Yet we don't know how to shun it. It is forced on us by our economic system as the alternative to starvation. It is also forced on us by an internal defect in the soul, by the feeling that in property may lie the germs of self-development and of exquisite or heroic deeds. Our life on earth is, and ought to be, material and carnal. But we have not yet learned to manage our materialism and carnality prop-

---

[5] Canute (994-1035), king and conqueror of all England, Denmark, and Norway, is said to have had his throne moved to the seashore where he attempted to make the tides obey him. Alexander the Great (356-323 B. C.), who succeeded before his early death in overcoming most of the Eastern Mediterranean area and Western Asia, is traditionally thought to have desired to conquer the whole world.

[6] Sonnet 129: 1, 12.

erly; they are still entangled with the desire for ownership, where (in the words of Dante) "Possession is one with loss."[7]

And this brings us to our fourth and final point: the blackberries.

Blackberries are not plentiful in this meagre grove, but they are easily seen from the public footpath which traverses it, and all too easily gathered. Foxgloves, too—people will pull up the foxgloves, and ladies of an educational tendency even grub for toadstools to show them on the Monday in class. Other ladies, less educated, roll down the bracken in the arms of their gentlemen friends. There is paper, there are tins. Pray, does my wood belong to me or doesn't it? And, if it does, should I not own it best by allowing no one else to walk there? There is a wood near Lyme Regis, also cursed by a public footpath, where the owner has not hesitated on this point. He had built high stone walls each side of the path, and has spanned it by bridges, so that the public circulate like termites while he gorges on the blackberries unseen. He really does own his wood, this able chap. Dives in Hell did pretty well, but the gulf dividing him from Lazarus could be traversed by vision,[8] and nothing traverses it here. And perhaps I shall come to this in time. I shall wall in and fence out until I really taste the sweets of property. Enormously stout, endlessly avaricious, pseudo-creative, intensely selfish, I shall weave upon my forehead the quadruple crown of possession until those nasty Bolshies come and take it off again and thrust me aside into the outer darkness.

---

[7] Possibly a reference to *The Convivio*, IV. x-xii.
[8] Luke 16: 19-31.

# IN PRAISE OF IGNORANCE

## Hilaire Belloc

Hilaire Belloc (1870-1953), born in Paris of Anglo-French parentage, began his literary career as soon as he received his degree from Oxford. A close friend of G. K. Chesterton, he was the author of essays, novels, historical works, and poems. He is well known also for his social and political writings and his engaging children's books. Belloc can write amusingly and at the same time profoundly "on nothing."

This essay appeared originally in New Statesman (June 7, 1930) and is reprinted from A Conversation with a Cat and Others (1931).

Erasmus wrote in praise of Folly.[1] I, coming exactly four hundred years after, would like to write in praise of Ignorance. I would like to write a little book about it, just as he did about Folly; but I am most unjustly handicapped. In the first place, I can't write what I like because we are not free, as the men of the Renaissance were free; in the second place, I haven't the time; in the third place, I haven't the talent. Still, I can at any rate write a little article in praise of Ignorance; and, so help me God, I will.

Remark the scope and amplitude of the affair! Let any man, however learned he may think himself, however varied his acquaintance with men, muck, money and the printed word, set down a list of subjects on which he could competently deal. Then let him compare it with the vast, the oceanic, prospect of the things of which he knows nothing. Nor let any man be humbled by this comparison. It is a great thing to possess a true knowledge of one's own ignorance, for in a sense you must have knowledge even to know the names of things which you do not know; as for instance, by pairs, Metabolism and Eutychianism, Isostatics and the Greater Lymphatics, Chron-

---

[1] Erasmus (1466?-1536), Dutch theologian and the greatest of Renaissance humanists, wrote the satirical Moriae encomium (The Praise of Folly, 1511).

ology and Entomology; to say nothing of Apology in the sense of arguments in defence of religious doctrine, for Apology to a Policeman is every man's affair.

You may take a list of countries of which you know the name and the shape on the map, but of themselves nothing at all; of towns, of persons—very great persons whose names are familiar to you, but beyond the name nothing.

To go back to the -ologies, examine yourself on Genealogy. What were the maiden names of Charlemagne's four great-grandmothers? Who is the rightful King of England at the present moment if (and here again glorious Ignorance intrudes) the supposed but doubtful will of Henry VIII still have force of law? What were the claims of the Spanish Infanta to that same throne of England at the end of the sixteenth century? And who was the father of Zebedee's children? Anyone could write down at top speed in half an hour more points of this kind on which he knew nothing than he could write down by laborious self-examination in a whole day similar points on which he had some little knowledge.

The modern system of examination (already menaced) has been very justly blamed by the wisest and the best. One of the less wise and not so good shall here say something in its favour. Anyone who has sat for an examination has had a vivid revelation of his own ignorance. I have written answers to perhaps a hundred examination papers in my time, and my attitude towards each of the wretched printed things as it lay before me (I being then surrounded by dozens of other victims each at his little desk, with an underpaid Invigilator glaring at us from a platform above) was one of violent bewilderment, loss of foothold, sinking into the abyss. I would see something like this: "Discuss the action of Berengarius at the Council of Blois." I knew vaguely what "Council" meant; I had been to Blois; but beyond that—stumped. Or again, "Give the principal attempts at the trisection of the plane angle by the epicycloidal method." I could not do so. Or again, much more straightforward, "Mention in their order the places visited by St. Paul in his nth missionary journey." Nothing doing.

I say that the soul receives great profit by correction of this kind. No man who has been examined but has at least come upon the knowledge of his own ignorance, which is the beginning of learning.

There are some, indeed, so stronghearted and so sane that they approach examinations daily from the very standpoint of ignorance, like those bluff travellers who, meeting the aristocracy of a foreign land, grin openly at them for mountebanks, keep their end up superbly in the vast saloons of Rome, of Warsaw, of Vienna, and go out contented with a smile yet broader than that which dignified their entrance. Of such was the young student of Divinity (later possessed of a cure of souls in the Isle of Man and quaintly affecting medieval customs) who, being set a certain examination paper to test his qualifications for Holy Orders, read its terms very carefully and discovered that of six questions he was to select three. Of those six questions one-half meant nothing to him whatsoever; they mentioned things of which he had no more heard than had the Colossians or Ephesians, or whoever they were,[2] of the first century yet heard of the Holy Ghost. But the other three contained each a word which he had heard before: he carefully put a little cross against each such question. They were as follows:

(1) What do you know of the Council of Chalcedon?
(2) Was Sozomen justified in his treatment of the Apollinarians?
(3) What is the distinction between the Cyprianic and the Augustinian attitude towards the Western Patriarchate?

He wrote each of these questions out in a fair, round, clerkly hand, leaving a little space below each. Then, in each of these spaces, he solemnly wrote, for the first the answer "Nothing"; for the second "No"; for the third "None." Having thus completed his paper, he went up and presented it to the Invigilator, bowed, and walked out. The fledgling clerics around him envied the facility of his erudition, the rapidity of his completed task, his early liberation into the happy sunlight of an Oxford June; but he was ploughed.

As is my most unfortunate foible in the discussion of any matter truly profound, I have allowed preliminaries to take up nearly all my space, and I have not as yet approached that chief spiritual attribute of Ignorance, which is its power to flood the mind with happiness. Ignorance is a very draught of beatitude. All the mystery and marvel

---

[2] They were Ephesians; Acts 19: 1-2.

of a wide champaign seen from a height at evening depends on our ignorance of the nasty people by which it is inhabited, their tortuous and sordid ways. All our loves, all our hero-worships, all our dreams of coming peace, all our visions of fortune, are the fruits of ignorance.

A man leaves a congenial company with whom he has held full communion. He goes off to take his train and thinks to have left behind him souls still vibrating in harmony with his own. They recollect him with a peaceful love. If they return to his name it is with murmurs of approbation. He rolls home satisfied. But the root of his happiness lies deep in ignorance, for hardly had he shut the door behind him when one of them said, "Does he still drink?" And another, "Yes, but he's got to that stage when he doesn't show it." And a third, "That's the most dangerous time!"

Nay, to conclude upon a note of grandeur, it is by Ignorance alone that we advance through the rough seas of this our mortal life. (The metaphor is not original; I do not claim it so; I copy it from others.) Were not men ignorant of what lay before them, no one would face the adventure. I knew one man, indeed, who was quite offensively stupid, dressed in a sort of purple-grey, and had himself so groomed and set up that he looked like the Successful Business Man of the Advertisements—which, indeed, he was. This man told me during a public luncheon that he had found life increasingly pleasant, and that in every fresh stage of it he discovered a further satisfaction. Now, I am glad to say that within twenty-four hours he was shot out of his motor-car and broke upon the sacred flints of England that prominent jaw which he had so abominably abused. Never more would he boast; or at least, not without a horrid mumbling.

In consideration of all this, I thank God for my own Ignorance, and though it is unfortunately less than that of most people, I flatter myself it will serve.

# THE CALAMITY OF APPOMATTOX

## H. L. Mencken

H. L. Mencken (1880-1956), from his editorial seat on the
Baltimore Sun, a daily paper in the city of his birth, and on
such magazines as Smart Set and American Mercury, rejoiced
in damning hypocrisy and complacency in American life.
His delight in iconoclasm and in the pyrotechnic use of
language infuses his scholarly The American Language, first
published in 1919, and numerous volumes of essays, including a series of six characteristically entitled Prejudices.

This essay appeared originally in American Mercury (September 1930) and is reprinted from A Mencken Chrestomathy
(1949).

No American historian, so far as I know, has ever tried to work out
the probable consequences if Grant instead of Lee had been on the
hot spot at Appomattox. How long would the victorious Confederacy
have endured? Could it have surmounted the difficulties inherent in
the doctrine of States' Rights, so often inconvenient and even
paralyzing to it during the war? Could it have remedied its plain
economic deficiencies, and become a self-sustaining nation? How
would it have protected itself against such war heroes as Beauregard
and Longstreet, Joe Wheeler and Nathan B. Forrest? And what
would have been its relations to the United States, socially, economically, spiritually and politically?

I am inclined, on all these counts, to be optimistic. The chief
evils in the Federal victory lay in the fact, from which we still suffer
abominably, that it was a victory of what we now call Babbitts over
what used to be called gentlemen. I am not arguing here, of course,
that the whole Confederate army was composed of gentlemen; on
the contrary, it was chiefly made up, like the Federal army, of innocent and unwashed peasants, and not a few of them got into its

corps of officers. But the impulse behind it, as everyone knows, was essentially aristocratic, and that aristocratic impulse would have fashioned the Confederacy if the fortunes of war had run the other way. Whatever the defects of the new commonwealth below the Potomac, it would have at least been a commonwealth founded upon a concept of human inequality, and with a superior minority at the helm. It might not have produced any more Washingtons, Madisons, Jeffersons, Calhouns and Randolphs of Roanoke, but it would certainly not have yielded itself to the Heflins, Caraways, Bilbos and Tillmans.[1]

The rise of such bounders was a natural and inevitable consequence of the military disaster. That disaster left the Southern gentry deflated and almost helpless. Thousands of the best young men among them had been killed, and thousands of those who survived came North. They commonly did well in the North, and were good citizens. My own native town of Baltimore was greatly enriched by their immigration, both culturally, and materially; if it is less corrupt today than most other large American cities, then the credit belongs largely to Virginians, many of whom arrived with no baggage save good manners and empty bellies. Back home they were sorely missed. First the carpetbaggers ravaged the land, and then it fell into the hands of the native white trash, already so poor that war and Reconstruction could not make them any poorer. When things began to improve they seized whatever was seizable, and their heirs and assigns, now poor no longer, hold it to this day. A raw plutocracy owns and operates the New South, with no challenge save from a proletariat, white and black, that is still three-fourths peasant, and hence too stupid to be dangerous. The aristocracy is almost extinct, at least as a force in government. It may survive in backwaters and on puerile levels, but of the men who run the South today, and represent it at Washington, not 5 percent, by any Southern standard, are gentlemen.

If the war had gone with the Confederates no such vermin would be in the saddle, nor would there be any sign below the Potomac of their chief contributions to American *Kultur*—Ku Kluxry,

---

[1] J. Thomas Heflin, Thaddeus H. Caraway, Theodore G. Bilbo, and John N. Tillman had risen from humble agrarian origins to high governmental positions (respectively as Senator from Alabama, Senator from Arkansas, Governor of Mississippi, and Member of Congress from Arkansas), in which they gained nation-wide notoriety in the 1920's for their demagogic advocacy of the cause of the poor whites and for their vehement anti-Negro, anti-Catholic views.

political ecclesiasticism, nigger-baiting, and the more homicidal variety of wowserism. Such things might have arisen in America, but they would not have arisen in the South. The old aristocracy, however degenerate it might have become, would have at least retained sufficient decency to see to that. New Orleans, today, would still be a highly charming and civilized (if perhaps somewhat zymotic) city, with a touch of Paris and another of Port Said. Charleston, which even now sprouts lady authors, would also sprout political philosophers. The University of Virginia would be what Jefferson intended it to be, and no shouting Methodist would haunt its campus. Richmond would be, not the dull suburb of nothing that it is now, but a beautiful and consoling second-rate capital, comparable to Budapest, Brussels, Stockholm or The Hague. And all of us, with the Middle West pumping its revolting silo juices into the East and West alike, would be making frequent leaps over the Potomac, to drink the sound red wine there and breathe the free air.

My guess is that the two Republics would be getting on pretty amicably. Perhaps they'd have come to terms as early as 1898, and fought the Spanish-American War together. In 1917 the confiding North might have gone out to save the world for democracy, but the South, vaccinated against both Wall Street and the Liberal whim-wham,[2] would have kept aloof—and maybe rolled up a couple of billions of profit from the holy crusade. It would probably be far richer today, independent, than it is with the clutch of the Yankee mortgage-shark still on its collar. It would be getting and using his money just the same, but his toll would be less. As things stand, he not only exploits the South economically; he also pollutes and debases it spiritually. It suffers damnably from low wages, but it suffers even more from the Chamber of Commerce metaphysic.

No doubt the Confederates, victorious, would have abolished slavery by the middle 80s. They were headed that way before the war, and the more sagacious of them were all in favor of it. But they were in favor of it on sound economic grounds, and not on the brummagem moral grounds which persuaded the North. The difference here is immense. In human history a moral victory is always a disaster, for it debauches and degrades both the victor and the van-

[2] A fantastic notion.

quished. The triumph of sin in 1865 would have stimulated and helped to civilize both sides.

Today the way out looks painful and hazardous. Civilization in the United States survives only in the big cities, and many of them— notably Boston and Philadelphia—seem to be sliding down to the cow country level. No doubt this standardization will go on until a few of the more resolute towns, headed by New York, take to open revolt, and try to break out of the Union. Already, indeed, it is talked of. But it will be hard to accomplish, for the tradition that the Union is indissoluble is now firmly established. If it had been broken in 1865 life would be far pleasanter today for every American of any noticeable decency. There are, to be sure, advantages in Union for everyone, but it must be manifest that they are greatest for the worst kinds of people. All the benefit that a New Yorker gets out of Kansas is no more than what he might get out of Saskatchewan, the Argentine pampas, or Siberia. But New York to a Kansan is not only a place where he may get drunk, look at dirty shows and buy bogus antiques; it is also a place where he may enforce his dunghill ideas upon his betters.

# SEED CORN AND MISTLETOE

## Bernard DeVoto

Bernard DeVoto (1897-1955) was born in Utah of Italian and
Mormon parentage and was educated at Harvard. For a short
time an editor of the Saturday Review of Literature, he also
wrote, between 1935 and 1952, "The Easy Chair," a regular
column in Harper's Magazine. He was the author of novels
and criticism, and was an authority on the history, literature,
and traditions of America, especially of primitive America and
the frontier.

This essay appeared originally in "The Easy Chair,"
Harper's Magazine (December 1936) and is reprinted from
Minority Report (1940).

No one can approach through winter darkness a house from whose
windows light shines out on the snow without feeling quieted and
heartened. Psychic subtleties may be active in such a response, but
there is no need to invoke them; for the obvious facts provide all
the explanation we require. A house means warmth and shelter, light
means human society. Snow and the dark have simplified the detail
of the picture and deadened sound—they suggest tranquillity, which
may mean much at the end of the day, and food or drink for restora-
tion, and the talk of friends or family. The human mind is addicted
to symbolism, and here is an image of ease, comfort, and reassurance
that speaks directly to us in early childhood and from then on. . . .
It is likely that very few people seeing a light on snow and quickening
to the thought of warmth within pause to inquire whether the
warmth comes from a gas furnace controlled by a thermostat or from
the hickory logs burning on a spacious hearth to which a poetic sense
would more properly attribute it. The light shining on the snow is
quite as beautiful and quite as heartening when power to furnish it
has been carried along a hundred miles of copper wire and stepped
down through a transformer as when it comes from a candle dipped
by hand.

Somewhere here is a text for a sermon, and sermons are appropriate to Christmas time, though with the clergy currently talking about a planned economy which will plow them under altogether, they may have to be preached by laymen. And everything about Christmas fares badly among the cerebral, who deplore its clearly reactionary nature, mutter about its vulgarization by trade and commerce, protest against its evil effects on children, and complain that it isn't what it used to be anyway and never can be again. Let us deal with these indignations first; for though the cerebral are always running a slight temperature on logical grounds, if the winter festival does indeed constitute a menace to society even a lay pulpit should take notice of it.

About the children. There are no statistical tables to tell us how many of them are still being deceived with an old and probably capitalistic myth called Santa Claus. Probably millions of them, for the mass of mankind has a gratifying disregard of theory, and parents continue, in spite of the heroic labors of educational psychologists, to deceive their children because they themselves were deceived a generation ago, remember liking it, and observe that their children like it too. The myth offends both a moral theory which holds that it is wrong to lie to children about anything and a highly scientific one which holds that you must not confuse a child's sense of reality by adding to his difficulty in dealing with real things the further difficulty of dealing with the altogether fictitious. Yet everyone knows that a child's sense of reality is quite incommensurable with an adult's and that children will make up phantasies of their own to supply the lack of any that may not be given them by others. The people who object to lying to children about Santa Claus must perforce lie to them about all the daily phenomena of existence, if indeed it is possible to say what a lie to a child is. And the very people who object to Santa Claus as a myth are prone to instruct them in such conceptions as human brotherhood, justice, and the classless society.

Both objections are on the level of the nostalgia which feels that the festival was all right for children when they themselves strung popcorn and cranberries to make decorations for the tree instead of the machine-made tinsel of to-day (but if that was Group Participation, was it not also Child Labor?), and that colored electric

lights are tawdry whereas little candles once had a simple purity—
it apparently being all right to burn the house up on Christmas Day
so long as you keep the festival simple and pure. This is on the same
level with that other sentiment of the thoughtful which sets out to
make wars impossible, along with racketeering and unfair competi-
tion, by keeping toy guns, cannon, and lead soldiers out of the hands
of children. Beat the toy sword into a toy steam-shovel, the notion
goes, and you will turn the child forever to the ways of peace, at
whatever cost of overproduction in the heavy industries. But if you
do not permit the normal warlike phantasies of the child a normal
expression at the right time you head straight for trouble. Either
you will render him unfit for normal aggression later on, thus making
him an easy prey for the combative, or you will insure such
phantasies getting an abnormal and delayed expression, thus making
war inevitable.

The unregarding behavior of untheoretical people is certainly
sounder. They act on an assumption that the important thing is to
make children happy. If you can give a child an experience of
authentic awe and wonder and anticipation by telling him that a
mythical fat man with a kind heart brings presents to children, why,
the thing that counts is giving him the experience. If children like
to play with toy guns, who is harmed? And if a child catches his
breath in ecstasy because here in the living room stands an evergreen
that has blossomed with colored lights, why that is everything in
itself. You have given the child an experience of ecstasy, which needs
neither justification nor analysis on logical principles.

One is constrained to be equally skeptical of the indignation that
sees Christmas as a conspiracy against the public peace and interest
by people who have Christmas presents to sell. Like so many other
causes of the cerebral, this presents itself as a benevolent champion-
ship of the exploited, whereas it is really a contempt of the common
man. It is the old, old cry of Utopians: the people are fools. The
people, that is, are weak, gullible, infatuated, unstable, venal, too
foolish to follow after righteousness—give us machine guns and we
will make them virtuous. A cerebral dictatorship, ever so kindly but
quite firm, would safeguard them from exploitation by the hucksters,
defend them from the seductions of advertising, deliver them from
the pumped-up hysteria of crowds. How pitiful that they should give

one another presents because the department store tells them to, how intolerable that the System should make money from a sentiment that the people only think they feel! See how mechanically the common man jerks about on his wire and how slavishly he does what he is told to do by conspirators in the service of commerce. Therefore let us save him from himself, teach him that his emotions are not his own, and deliver him into self-knowledge and emancipation—at the point of a bayonet. . . . A lay pulpit must denounce all this fervor as propaganda—fascist or communist, whichever epithet will most affront the kindly theorist. It is an ancient despair uttering an ancient cry, the lust of the fretted to save the people by force. The people should ignore it altogether.

As of course they do. They go on giving one another presents at Christmas time no matter how the profits of the hucksters may pile up. They spend as much as they can afford to, and usually a good deal more. If trade prospers and the banks can express Christmas in the form of graphs, the public is not appalled. Nor is its feeling degraded. The cathedrals of the age of faith, which the theories treat with the greatest respect, were fenced round by the booths of traders, and an earlier Christianity managed to combine a good deal of commerce with its devotion—and the roads to the American camp-meeting were thronged with peddlers whom the devout patronized without in the least diminishing their pious exercises. Not the trading booths but the devotion was the important thing about the cathedrals, and the important thing about Christmas is not that the people are sold presents but that they give them to one another. The most diverse and even the most irrelevant motives may enter in, many of them doubtless a good deal less than ideal; but the principal one, the one without which none of the others could possibly operate, is the human warmth of friends and relatives seeking expression and finding it. Christmas may be commercialized till it has become indispensable to the business system and vulgarized till a sensitive theory shudders when dealing with it, but people go on making gifts to those who are dear to them. The custom has the natural force of a stream flowing and takes its curve as a stream does, from its own nature. It is the popular fulfillment of human need and desire. The people behave that way, and you can do nothing whatever about them.

That is the firstly of a lay sermon. The secondly goes on to point out how, though in the American Christmas are recognizable many elements taken from many places, the whole is something altogether in its own terms. Our Christmas Eve is English and our Christmas morning looks very German. The carols sung in our churches and streets (and, to advertise soap or engine oil, in our broadcasting studios, a native touch probably loathsome to the sensitive) come from all over Europe but are French to a functional anthropologist, and medieval French at that. A good many of the conventional symbols are Asiatic, and the firecrackers which children set off in San Francisco and New Orleans exorcise demons and propitiate gods that are clearly Chinese. The mistletoe is Norse, and a vigilant suspicion, observing the holly and the eggnog, can detect compulsions bubbling in the blood of pagans far older than the rise of that star in the East which they are used to commemorate. Yes, a hodgepodge of rituals and symbols and of beliefs gathered at random, but it has taken a shape of its own which no one who has experienced it can ever possibly confuse with any other Christmas. One who has known the American Christmas as a child, a lover, or a parent knows a festival which has shaped his thought and patterns of emotion lying far deeper than thought, in a way uniquely its own. In whatever corner of the earth he may find himself on Christmas Eve, the rhythms pulsing in his nerves and the images translating them will have reference to the common and unique experience of Americans. That remembered, remembering child seeing the filled stocking and the lighted tree, hearing a Catholic carol so illogically sung in a Congregational meetinghouse, hurrying to deliver a holly wreath to a friend of his parents in order to try his skates the sooner on the ice of country pond or city sidewalk—is set off from all foreign children in things remembered and things experienced. An American tradition, different from all other traditions, has created its own symbols.

There are a good many like them, and a lay preacher would call them into remembrance at Christmas, a time dedicated from its origin to remembering the justifications of hopefulness and disregarding the foundations of despair. Autumn comes and the President of the United States summons the nation to render formal thanks for its harvest, and lesser magistrates repeat his proclamation. Meanwhile at half the farm doorways in New England pumpkins stand on the stoop, a splash of color against the dulling landscape, though no one can explain the custom. In rural places across the continent boys nail on the barn door the tails of woodchucks and chipmunks and red squirrels they have shot; beside them, and on the walls of garages in the towns, their fathers add last year's automobile-license plates to the column of those that have gone before. Seed corn hangs in bunches on the wall that gets the sun, and the corn is shocked. The corn is shocked to dry, and so is the wheat, and the form and structure of the shocking are peculiar to the United States. We shock our corn differently, and the image also calls up associations unique to Americans; for it is part of an intricate organization of skills and customs and emotions, of social beliefs and relationships, of a way of living with and in society that is our own way and no one else's. A live symbol to Americans, and one whose meaning is beyond the instinct and out of the comprehension of all other people.

A symbol of an American way of life. Let it be remembered at Christmas time, and with it a great company of its kind, since Christmas is a time for symbols. Light shining on snow through winter dark is as universal as the star going before the Wise Men on their way, but also to all who have lived in America it has a special reference, being as well the light from a cabin in the clearing with the forest beyond them stretching toward the unknown West. Few Americans now have ever lived in a cabin or ever seen a clearing in the forest, yet the words mean something to them that they mean to no one else on earth. Fewer still have ever ridden in a stagecoach climbing toward Cumberland Gap, or plodded beside a canvas-covered wagon toward the land where the streams sink out of sight, with Indians possibly crouching behind the next rise. It is a long time since a mythical Indian princess interceded for a probably lying Captain John Smith; none of us has driven the Sovereign of the Seas round the Horn to beat the clipper fleet; none of us has ridden down the Natchez Trace or forced a plow for the first time through matted grass roots to prairie soil; Andrew Jackson and Abe Lincoln and Buffalo Bill and Daniel Boone are dead. Huck Finn is only someone in a book, and Paul Bunyan is not even that but only talk sleepy at best and now no longer uttered. But though none of us ever saw the Wise Men coming from the East, we still make gifts to our friends and children on Christmas Day. And the cabin in the clearing, the clipper fleet, the departed heroes, and the corn standing in shocks are systolic in us, part of the rhythm of our breath and of our desire—and part too of our fate. They stand for our own way of life, they are our living tradition; and we understand them, being shaped by them and being inescapably obedient to them, and no one else understands them. That is the way our corn is shocked.

That may as well be remembered at Christmas time, at Christmas time especially in a period of tribulation. The cerebral—people characterized primarily by fear and by contempt of the unconsidered multitudes and by a lust for absolutes and for absolute power—tell us that America must choose between two ways of life, both European, both essentially the same, both intolerable. Let there be read to them the prayer appointed to be read in churches on Christmas Day: they are fools and liars and the truth is not in them. That is not our choice but an alien one, and our choice is foreordained for us by our own tradition; our native way of life formed by our own systole and diastole. Our corn is maize, and Europe had no maize.

# SEX EX MACHINA

## James Thurber

James Thurber was born in 1894 in Ohio and educated there.
In 1926, at the suggestion of E. B. White, he became associated, as humorist and cartoonist, with The New Yorker
magazine. He has maintained the connection and also has a
thriving independent reputation for his volumes of essays,
fables, and cartoons. The attitude in most of his work, that
of the "little man" baffled by the intricacies of modern
technology and victimized by high-pressure salesmanship and
bureaucratic government, produces whimsical yet serious
criticism.

This essay appeared originally in The New Yorker (March
13, 1937) and is reprinted from Let Your Mind Alone!
(1937).

With the disappearance of the gas mantle and the advent of the
short circuit, man's tranquillity began to be threatened by everything
he put his hand on. Many people believe that it was a sad day indeed
when Benjamin Franklin tied that key to a kite string and flew the
kite in a thunderstorm; other people believe that if it hadn't been
Franklin, it would have been someone else. As, of course, it was in
the case of the harnessing of steam and the invention of the gas
engine. At any rate, it has come about that so-called civilized man
finds himself today surrounded by the myriad mechanical devices of
a technological world. Writers of books on how to control your
nerves, how to conquer fear, how to cultivate calm, how to be happy
in spite of everything, are of several minds as regards the relation of
man and the machine. Some of them are prone to believe that the
mind and body, if properly disciplined, can get the upper hand of
this mechanized existence. Others merely ignore the situation and
go on to the profitable writing of more facile chapters of inspiration.

Still others attribute the whole menace of the machine to sex, and so confuse the average reader that he cannot always be certain whether he has been knocked down by an automobile or is merely in love.

Dr. Bisch,[1] the Be-Glad-You're-Neurotic man, has a remarkable chapter which deals, in part, with man, sex, and the machine. He examines the case of three hypothetical men who start across a street on a red light and get in the way of an oncoming automobile. A dodges successfully; B stands still, "accepting the situation with calm and resignation," thus becoming one of my favorite heroes in modern belles-lettres; and C hesitates, wavers, jumps backward and forward, and finally runs head on into the car. To lead you through Dr. Bisch's complete analysis of what was wrong with B and C would occupy your whole day. He mentions what the McDougallians [2] would say ("Instinct!"), what the Freudians would retort ("Complexes!"), and what the behaviorists would shout ("Conditioned reflexes!"). He also brings in what the physiologists would say— deficient thyroid, hypoadrenal functioning, and so on. The average sedentary man of our time who is at all suggestible must emerge from this chapter believing that his chances of surviving a combination of instinct, complexes, reflexes, glands, sex, and present-day traffic conditions are about equal to those of a one-legged blind man trying to get out of a labyrinth.

Let us single out what Dr. Bisch thinks the Freudians would say about poor Mr. C, who ran right into the car. He writes, " 'Sex hunger,' the Freudians would declare. 'Always keyed up and irritable because of it. Undoubtedly suffers from insomnia and when he does sleep his dream life must be productive, distorted, and possibly frightening. Automobile unquestionably has sex significance for him . . . to C the car is both enticing and menacing at one and the same time. . . . A thorough analysis is indicated. . . . It might take months. But then, the man needs an analysis as much as food. He is heading for a complete nervous collapse.' " It is my studied opinion, not to

---

[1] Dr. Louis E. Bisch (1885-    ), American neuropsychiatrist and popularizer of Freudian theory; author of books and articles, including *Be Glad You're Neurotic* (1936).

[2] McDougallians are followers of William McDougall (1871-1938), professor of psychology at Harvard and Duke, who believed that man strives for biologically valuable ends because he is equipped by instinct to pursue actions that will safeguard the species.

put too fine a point on it, that Mr. C is heading for a good mangling, and that if he gets away with only a nervous collapse, it will be a miracle.

I have not always, I am sorry to say, been able to go the whole way with the Freudians, or even a very considerable distance. Even though, as Dr. Bisch says, "One must admit that the Freudians have had the best of it thus far. At least they have received the most publicity." It is in matters like their analysis of men and machines, of Mr. C and the automobile, that the Freudians and I part company. Of course, the analysis above is simply Dr. Bisch's idea of what the Freudians would say, but I think he has got it down pretty well. Dr. Bisch himself leans toward the Freudian analysis of Mr. C, for he says in this same chapter, "An automobile bearing down upon you may be a sex symbol at that, you know, especially if you dream it." It is my contention, of course, that even if you dream it, it is probably not a sex symbol, but merely an automobile bearing down upon you. And if it bears down upon you in real life, I am sure it is an automobile. I have seen the same behavior that characterized Mr. C displayed by a squirrel (Mr. S) that lives in the grounds of my house in the country. He is a fairly tame squirrel, happily mated and not sex-hungry, if I am any judge, but nevertheless he frequently runs out toward my automobile when I start down the driveway, and then hesitates, wavers, jumps forward and backward, and occasionally would run right into the car except that he is awfully fast on his feet and that I always hurriedly put on the brakes of the 1935 V-8 Sex Symbol that I drive.

I have seen this same behavior in the case of rabbits (notoriously uninfluenced by any sex symbols save those of other rabbits), dogs, pigeons, a doe, a young hawk (which flew at my car), a blue heron that I encountered on a country road in Vermont, and once, near Paul Smith's in the Adirondacks, a fox. They all acted exactly like Mr. C. The hawk, unhappily, was killed. All the others escaped with nothing worse, I suppose, than a complete nervous collapse. Although I cannot claim to have been conversant with the private life and the secret compulsions, the psychoneuroses and the glandular activities of all these animals, it is nevertheless my confident and unswervable belief that there was nothing at all the matter with any one of them. Like Mr. C, they suddenly saw a car swiftly bearing down upon them, got excited, and lost their heads. I do not believe, you see, there was anything the matter with Mr. C, either. But I do believe that, after a thorough analysis lasting months, with a lot of harping on the incident of the automobile, something might very well come to be the matter with him. He might even actually get to suffering from the delusion that he believes automobiles are sex symbols.

It seems to me worthy of note that Dr. Bisch, in reciting the reactions of three persons in the face of an oncoming car, selected three men. What would have happened had they been Mrs. A, Mrs. B, and Mrs. C? You know as well as I do: all three of them would have hesitated, wavered, jumped forward and backward, and finally run head on into the car if some man hadn't grabbed them. (I used to know a motorist who, every time he approached a woman standing on a curb preparing to cross the street, shouted, "Hold it, stupid!") It is not too much to say that, with a car bearing down upon them, ninety-five women out of a hundred would act like Mr. C—or Mr. S, the squirrel, or Mr. F, the fox. But it is certainly too much to say that ninety-five out of every hundred women look upon an automobile as a sex symbol. For one thing, Dr. Bisch points out that the automobile serves as a sex symbol because of the "mechanical principle involved." But only one woman in a thousand really knows anything about the mechanical principle involved in an automobile. And yet, as I have said, ninety-five out of a hundred would hesitate, waver, and jump, just as Mr. C did. I think we have the Freudians here. If we haven't proved our case with rabbits and a blue heron, we have certainly proved it with women.

To my notion, the effect of the automobile and of other mechanical contrivances on the state of our nerves, minds, and spirits is a problem which the popular psychologists whom I have dealt with know very little about. The sexual explanation of the relationship of man and the machine is not good enough. To arrive at the real explanation, we have to begin very far back, as far back as Franklin and the kite, or at least as far back as a certain man and woman who appear in a book of stories written more than sixty years ago by Max Adeler.[3] One story in this book tells about a housewife who bought

---

[3] Max Adeler is the pen name of Charles Heber Clark (1841-1915), author of *Out of the Hurly-Burly; or Life in an Odd Corner* (1874), a collection of sketches, one of which concerns the convertible ironing board (Chap. 2).

a combination ironing board and card table, which some New England genius had thought up in his spare time. The husband, coming home to find the devilish contraption in the parlor, was appalled. "What is that thing?" he demanded. His wife explained that it was a card table, but that if you pressed a button underneath, it would become an ironing board. Whereupon she pushed the button and the table leaped a foot into the air, extended itself, and became an ironing board. The story goes on to tell how the thing finally became so finely sensitized that it would change back and forth if you merely touched it—you didn't have to push the button. The husband stuck it in the attic (after it had leaped up and struck him a couple of times while he was playing euchre), and on windy nights it could be heard flopping and banging around, changing from a card table to an ironing board and back. The story serves as one example of our dread heritage of annoyance, shock, and terror arising out of the nature of mechanical contrivances *per se*. The mechanical principle involved in this damnable invention had, I believe, no relationship to sex whatsoever. There are certain analysts who see sex in anything, even a leaping ironing board, but I think we can ignore these scientists.

No man (to go on) who has wrestled with a self-adjusting card table can ever be quite the man he once was. If he arrives at the state where he hesitates, wavers, and jumps at every mechanical device he encounters, it is not, I submit, because he recognizes the enticements of sex in the device, but only because he recognizes the menace of the machine as such. There might very well be, in every descendant of the man we have been discussing, an inherited desire to jump at, and conquer, mechanical devices before they have a chance to turn into something twice as big and twice as menacing. It is not reasonable to expect that his children and their children will have entirely escaped the stigma of such traumata. I myself will never be the man I once was, nor will my descendants probably ever amount to much, because of a certain experience I had with an automobile.

I had gone out to the barn of my country place, a barn which was used both as a garage and a kennel, to quiet some large black poodles. It was 1 A.M. of a pitch-dark night in winter and the poodles had apparently been terrified by some kind of a prowler, a tramp, a turtle, or perhaps a fiend of some sort. Both my poodles and I myself believed, at the time, in fiends, and still do. Fiends who materialize out of nothing and nowhere, like winged pigweed or Russian thistle. I had quite a time quieting the dogs, because their panic spread to me and mine spread back to them again, in a kind of vicious circle. Finally, a hush as ominous as their uproar fell upon them, but they kept looking over their shoulders, in a kind of apprehensive way. "There's nothing to be afraid of," I told them as firmly as I could, and just at that moment the klaxon [4] of my car, which was just behind me, began to shriek. Everybody has heard a klaxon on a car suddenly begin to sound; I understand it is a short circuit that causes it. But very few people have heard one scream behind them while they were quieting six or eight alarmed poodles in the middle of the night in an old barn. I jump now whenever I hear a klaxon, even the klaxon on my own car when I push the button intentionally. The experience has left its mark. Everybody, from the day of the jumping card table to the day of the screaming klaxon, has had similar shocks. You can see the result, entirely unsuperinduced by sex, in the strained faces and muttering lips of people who pass you on the streets of great, highly mechanized cities. There goes a man who picked up one of those trick matchboxes that whir in your hands; there goes a woman who tried to change a fuse without turning off the current; and yonder toddles an ancient who cranked an old Reo with the spark advanced. Every person carries in his consciousness the old scar, or the fresh wound, of some harrowing misadventure with a contraption of some sort. I know people who would not deposit a nickel and a dime in a cigarette-vending machine and push the lever even if a diamond necklace came out. I know dozens who would not climb into an airplane even if it didn't move off the ground. In none of these people have I discerned what I would call a neurosis, an "exaggerated" fear; I have discerned only a natural caution in a world made up of gadgets that whir and whine and whiz and shriek and sometimes explode.

I should like to end with the case history of a friend of mine in Ohio named Harvey Lake. When he was only nineteen, the steering bar of an old electric runabout broke off in his hand, causing the

---

[4] See footnote 2 to the essay "A Lost Wood."

machine to carry him through a fence and into the grounds of the Columbus School for Girls. He developed a fear of automobiles, trains, and every other kind of vehicle that was not pulled by a horse. Now, the psychologists would call this a complex and represent the fear as abnormal, but I see it as a purely reasonable apprehension. If Harvey Lake had, because he was catapulted into the grounds of the Columbus School for Girls, developed a fear of girls, I would call that a complex; but I don't call his normal fear of machines a complex. Harvey Lake never in his life got into a plane (he died in a fall from a porch), but I do not regard that as neurotic, either, but only sensible.

I have, to be sure, encountered men with complexes. There was, for example, Marvin Belt. He had a complex about airplanes that was quite interesting. He was not afraid of machinery, or of high places, or of crashes. He was simply afraid that the pilot of any plane he got into might lose his mind. "I imagine myself high over Montana," he once said to me, "in a huge, perfectly safe tri-motored plane. Several of the passengers are dozing, others are reading, but I am keeping my eyes glued on the door to the cockpit. Suddenly the pilot steps out of it, a wild light in his eyes, and in a falsetto like that of a little girl he says to me, 'Conductor, will you please let me off at One-Hundred-and-Twenty-fifth Street?'" "But," I said to Belt, "even if the pilot does go crazy, there is still the co-pilot." "No, there isn't," said Belt. "The pilot has hit the co-pilot over the head with something and killed him." Yes, the psychoanalysts can have Marvin Belt. But they can't have Harvey Lake, or Mr. C, or Mr. S, or Mr. F, or, while I have my strength, me.

# ONCE MORE TO THE LAKE

## E. B. White

E. B. White was born in 1899 in Mt. Vernon, New York,
and has been a contributor to The New Yorker magazine
since the 1920's. Poet, essayist, critic, commentator on the
vagaries of local, national, and international affairs, he lived
in New York for many years but has lately made his home,
with his family, in Maine.

This essay, written in August 1941, appeared originally in
the section "One Man's Meat" in Harper's Magazine (October
1941) and is reprinted from the volume One Man's Meat
(new ed., 1944).

One summer, along about 1904, my father rented a camp on a lake
in Maine and took us all there for the month of August. We all got
ringworm from some kittens and had to rub Pond's Extract on our
arms and legs night and morning, and my father rolled over in a
canoe with all his clothes on; but outside of that the vacation was a
success and from then on none of us ever thought there was any place
in the world like that lake in Maine. We returned summer after
summer—always on August 1st for one month. I have since become
a salt-water man, but sometimes in summer there are days when the
restlessness of the tides and the fearful cold of the sea water and
the incessant wind which blows across the afternoon and into the
evening make me wish for the placidity of a lake in the woods. A few
weeks ago this feeling got so strong I bought myself a couple of bass
hooks and a spinner and returned to the lake where we used to go,
for a week's fishing and to revisit old haunts.

I took along my son, who had never had any fresh water up his
nose and who had seen lily pads only from train windows. On the
journey over to the lake I began to wonder what it would be like. I
wondered how time would have marred this unique, this holy spot—
the coves and streams, the hills that the sun set behind, the camps

and the paths behind the camps. I was sure that the tarred road would have found it out and I wondered in what other ways it would be desolated. It is strange how much you can remember about places like that once you allow your mind to return into the grooves which lead back. You remember one thing, and that suddenly reminds you of another thing. I guess I remembered clearest of all the early mornings, when the lake was cool and motionless, remembered how the bedroom smelled of the lumber it was made of and of the wet woods whose scent entered through the screen. The partitions in the camp were thin and did not extend clear to the top of the rooms, and as I was always the first up I would dress softly so as not to wake the others, and sneak out into the sweet outdoors and start out in the canoe, keeping close along the shore in the long shadows of the pines. I remembered being very careful never to rub my paddle against the gunwale for fear of disturbing the stillness of the cathedral.

The lake had never been what you would call a wild lake. There were cottages sprinkled around the shores, and it was in farming country although the shores of the lake were quite heavily wooded. Some of the cottages were owned by nearby farmers, and you would live at the shore and eat your meals at the farmhouse. That's what our family did. But although it wasn't wild, it was a fairly large and undisturbed lake and there were places in it which, to a child at least, seemed infinitely remote and primeval.

I was right about the tar: it led to within half a mile of the shore. But when I got back there, with my boy, and we settled into a camp near a farmhouse and into the kind of summertime I had known, I could tell that it was going to be pretty much the same as it had been before—I knew it, lying in bed the first morning, smelling the bedroom, and hearing the boy sneak quietly out and go off along the shore in a boat. I began to sustain the illusion that he was I, and therefore, by simple transposition, that I was my father. This sensation persisted, kept cropping up all the time we were there. It was not an entirely new feeling, but in this setting it grew much stronger. I seemed to be living a dual existence. I would be in the middle of some simple act, I would be picking up a bait box or laying down a table fork, or I would be saying something, and suddenly it would be not I but my father who was saying the words or making the gesture. It gave me a creepy sensation.

We went fishing the first morning. I felt the same damp moss covering the worms in the bait can, and saw the dragonfly alight on the tip of my rod as it hovered a few inches from the surface of the water. It was the arrival of this fly that convinced me beyond any doubt that everything was as it always had been, that the years were a mirage and there had been no years. The small waves were the same, chucking the rowboat under the chin as we fished at anchor, and the boat was the same boat, the same color green and the ribs broken in the same places, and under the floor-boards the same freshwater leavings and débris—the dead helgramite,[1] the wisps of moss, the rusty discarded fishhook, the dried blood from yesterday's catch. We stared silently at the tips of our rods, at the dragonflies that came and went. I lowered the tip of mine into the water, tentatively, pensively dislodging the fly, which darted two feet away, poised, darted two feet back, and came to rest again a little farther up the rod. There had been no years between the ducking of this dragonfly and the other one—the one that was part of memory. I looked at the boy, who was silently watching his fly, and it was my hands that held his rod, my eyes watching. I felt dizzy and didn't know which rod I was at the end of.

We caught two bass, hauling them in briskly as though they were mackerel, pulling them over the side of the boat in a businesslike manner without any landing net, and stunning them with a blow on the back of the head. When we got back for a swim before lunch, the lake was exactly where we had left it, the same number of inches from the dock, and there was only the merest suggestion of a breeze. This seemed an utterly enchanted sea, this lake you could leave to its own devices for a few hours and come back to, and find that it had not stirred, this constant and trustworthy body of water. In the shallows, the dark, water-soaked sticks and twigs, smooth and old, were undulating in clusters on the bottom against the clean ribbed sand, and the track of the mussel was plain. A school of minnows swam by, each minnow with its small individual shadow, doubling the attendance, so clear and sharp in the sunlight. Some of the other campers were in swimming, along the shore, one of them with a cake of soap, and the water felt thin and clear and unsubstantial. Over

---

[1] The nymph of the May-fly, an ephemerid, much used as fish bait.

the years there had been this person with the cake of soap, this cultist, and here he was. There had been no years.

Up to the farmhouse to dinner through the teeming, dusty field, the road under our sneakers was only a two-track road. The middle track was missing, the one with the marks of the hooves and the splotches of dried, flaky manure. There had always been three tracks to choose from in choosing which track to walk in; now the choice was narrowed down to two. For a moment I missed terribly the middle alternative. But the way led past the tennis court, and something about the way it lay there in the sun reassured me; the tape had loosened along the backline, the alleys were green with plantains and other weeds, and the net (installed in June and removed in September) sagged in the dry noon, and the whole place steamed with midday heat and hunger and emptiness. There was a choice of pie for dessert, and one was blueberry and one was apple, and the waitresses were the same country girls, there having been no passage of time, only the illusion of it as in a dropped curtain—the waitresses were still fifteen; their hair had been washed, that was the only difference—they had been to the movies and seen the pretty girls with the clean hair.

Summertime, oh summertime, pattern of life indelible, the fade-proof lake, the woods unshatterable, the pasture with the sweetfern and the juniper forever and ever, summer without end; this was the background, and the life along the shore was the design, the cottagers with their innocent and tranquil design, their tiny docks with the flagpole and the American flag floating against the white clouds in the blue sky, the little paths over the roots of the trees leading from camp to camp and the paths leading back to the outhouses and the can of lime for sprinkling, and at the souvenir counters at the store the miniature birch-bark canoes and the post cards that showed things looking a little better than they looked. This was the American family at play, escaping the city heat, wondering whether the newcomers in the camp at the head of the cove were "common" or "nice," wondering whether it was true that the people who drove up for Sunday dinner at the farmhouse were turned away because there wasn't enough chicken.

It seemed to me, as I kept remembering all this, that those times and those summers had been infinitely precious and worth saving.

There had been jollity and peace and goodness. The arriving (at the beginning of August) had been so big a business in itself, at the railway station the farm wagon drawn up, the first smell of the pine-laden air, the first glimpse of the smiling farmer, and the great importance of the trunks and your father's enormous authority in such matters, and the feel of the wagon under you for the long ten-mile haul, and at the top of the last long hill catching the first view of the lake after eleven months of not seeing this cherished body of water. The shouts and cries of the other campers when they saw you, and the trunks to be unpacked, to give up their rich burden. (Arriving was less exciting nowadays, when you sneaked up in your car and parked it under a tree near the camp and took out the bags and in five minutes it was all over, no fuss, no loud wonderful fuss about trunks.)

Peace and goodness and jollity. The only thing that was wrong now, really, was the sound of the place, an unfamiliar nervous sound of the outboard motors. This was the note that jarred, the one thing that would sometimes break the illusion and set the years moving. In those other summertimes all motors were inboard; and when they were at a little distance, the noise they made was a sedative, an in-gredient of summer sleep. They were one-cylinder and two-cylinder engines, and some were make-and-break and some were jump-spark, but they all made a sleepy sound across the lake. The one-lungers throbbed and fluttered, and the twin-cylinder ones purred and purred, and that was a quiet sound too. But now the campers all had out-boards. In the daytime, in the hot mornings, these motors made a petulant, irritable sound; at night, in the still evening when the after-glow lit the water, they whined about one's ears like mosquitoes. My boy loved our rented outboard, and his great desire was to achieve singlehanded mastery over it, and authority, and he soon learned the trick of choking it a little (but not too much), and the adjustment of the needle valve. Watching him I would remember the things you could do with the old one-cylinder engine with the heavy flywheel, how you could have it eating out of your hand if you got really close to it spiritually. Motor boats in those days didn't have clutches, and you would make a landing by shutting off the motor at the proper time and coasting in with a dead rudder. But there was a way of reversing them, if you learned the trick, by cutting the switch and putting it on again exactly on the final dying revolution of the fly-wheel, so that it would kick back against compression and begin reversing. Approaching a dock in a strong following breeze, it was difficult to slow up sufficiently by the ordinary coasting method, and if a boy felt he had complete mastery over his motor, he was tempted to keep it running beyond its time and then reverse it a few feet from the dock. It took a cool nerve, because if you threw the switch a twentieth of a second too soon you would catch the flywheel when it still had speed enough to go up past center, and the boat would leap ahead, charging bull-fashion at the dock.

We had a good week at the camp. The bass were biting well and the sun shone endlessly, day after day. We would be tired at night and lie down in the accumulated heat of the little bedrooms after the long hot day and the breeze would stir almost imperceptibly outside and the smell of the swamp drift in through the rusty screens. Sleep would come easily and in the morning the red squirrel would be on the roof, tapping out his gay routine. I kept remembering everything, lying in bed in the mornings—the small steamboat that had a long rounded stern like the lip of a Ubangi, and how quietly she ran on the moonlight sails, when the older boys played their mandolins and the girls sang and we ate doughnuts dipped in sugar, and how sweet the music was on the water in the shining night, and what it had felt like to think about girls then. After breakfast we would go up to the store and the things were in the same place— the minnows in a bottle, the plugs and spinners disarranged and pawed over by the youngsters from the boys' camp, the fig newtons and the Beeman's gum. Outside, the road was tarred and cars stood in front of the store. Inside, all was just as it had always been, except there was more Coca-Cola and not so much Moxie and root beer and birch beer and sarsaparilla. We would walk out with a bottle of pop apiece and sometimes the pop would backfire up our noses and hurt. We explored the streams, quietly, where the turtles slid off the sunny logs and dug their way into the soft bottom; and we lay on the town wharf and fed worms to the tame bass. Everywhere we went I had trouble making out which was I, the one walking at my side, the one walking in my pants.

One afternoon while we were there at that lake a thunderstorm came up. It was like the revival of an old melodrama that I had seen long ago with childish awe. The second-act climax of the drama of the electrical disturbance over a lake in America had not changed in any important respect. This was the big scene, still the big scene. The whole thing was so familiar, the first feeling of oppression and heat and a general air around camp of not wanting to go very far away. In midafternoon (it was all the same) a curious darkening of the sky, and a lull in everything that had made life tick; and then the way the boats suddenly swung the other way at their moorings with the coming of a breeze out of the new quarter, and the premonitory rumble. Then the kettle drum, then the snare, then the bass drum and cymbals, then crackling light against the dark, and the gods grinning and licking their chops in the hills. Afterward the calm, the rain steadily rustling in the calm lake, the return of light and hope and spirits, and the campers running out in joy and relief to go swimming in the rain, their bright cries perpetuating the deathless joke about how they were getting simply drenched, and the children screaming with delight at the new sensation of bathing in the rain, and the joke about getting drenched linking the generations in a strong indestructible chain. And the comedian who waded in carrying an umbrella.

When the others went swimming my son said he was going in too. He pulled his dripping trunks from the line where they had hung all through the shower, and wrung them out. Languidly, and with no thought of going in, I watched him, his hard little body, skinny and bare, saw him wince slightly as he pulled up around his vitals the small, soggy, icy garment. As he buckled the swollen belt suddenly my groin felt the chill of death.

# THE DEATH OF THE MOTH

## Virginia Woolf

Virginia Woolf (1882-1941), born in London and brought up in surroundings of intellectual brilliance, is considered among the best of modern novelists for her distinguished work in Jacob's Room (1922), Mrs. Dalloway (1925), and To the Lighthouse (1927). In these novels she explored varied modes of consciousness, especially (as she termed it) "the moment of being." Her method of developing the meaning of such a moment is best seen in some of her essays.

This essay is reprinted from The Death of the Moth and Other Essays (1942).

Moths that fly by day are not properly to be called moths; they do not excite that pleasant sense of dark autumn nights and ivy-blossom which the commonest yellow-underwing asleep in the shadow of the curtain never fails to rouse in us. They are hybrid creatures, neither gay like butterflies nor sombre like their own species. Nevertheless the present specimen, with his narrow hay-coloured wings, fringed with a tassel of the same colour, seemed to be content with life. It was a pleasant morning, mid-September, mild, benignant, yet with a keener breath than that of the summer months. The plough was already scoring the field opposite the window, and where the share had been, the earth was pressed flat and gleamed with moisture. Such vigour came rolling in from the fields and the down beyond that it was difficult to keep the eyes strictly turned upon the book. The rooks too were keeping one of their annual festivities; soaring round the tree tops until it looked as if a vast net with thousands of black knots in it had been cast up into the air; which, after a few moments sank slowly down upon the trees until every twig seemed to have a knot at the end of it. Then, suddenly, the net would be thrown into the air again in a wider circle this time, with the utmost clamour and vociferation, as though to be thrown into the air and settle slowly down upon the tree tops were a tremendously exciting experience.

The same energy which inspired the rooks, the ploughmen, the horses, and even, it seemed, the lean bare-backed downs, sent the moth fluttering from side to side of his square of the window-pane. One could not help watching him. One was, indeed, conscious of a queer feeling of pity for him. The possibilities of pleasure seemed that morning so enormous and so various that to have only a moth's part in life, and a day moth's at that, appeared a hard fate, and his zest in enjoying his meagre opportunities to the full, pathetic. He flew vigorously to one corner of his compartment, and, after waiting there a second, flew across to the other. What remained for him but to fly to a third corner and then to a fourth? That was all he could do, in spite of the size of the downs, the width of the sky, the far-off smoke of houses, and the romantic voice, now and then, of a steamer out at sea. What he could do he did. Watching him, it seemed as if a fibre, very thin but pure, of the enormous energy of the world had been thrust into his frail and diminutive body. As often as he crossed the pane, I could fancy that a thread of vital light became visible. He was little or nothing but life.

Yet, because he was so small, and so simple a form of the energy that was rolling in at the open window and driving its way through so many narrow and intricate corridors in my own brain and in those of other human beings, there was something marvellous as well as pathetic about him. It was as if someone had taken a tiny bead of pure life and decking it as lightly as possible with down and feathers, had set it dancing and zigzagging to show us the true nature of life. Thus displayed one could not get over the strangeness of it. One is apt to forget all about life, seeing it humped and bossed and garnished and cumbered so that it has to move with the greatest circumspection and dignity. Again, the thought of all that life might have been had he been born in any other shape caused one to view his simple activities with a kind of pity.

After a time, tired by his dancing apparently, he settled on the window ledge in the sun, and, the queer spectacle being at an end, I forgot about him. Then, looking up, my eye was caught by him. He was trying to resume his dancing, but seemed either so stiff or so awkward that he could only flutter to the bottom of the window-pane; and when he tried to fly across it he failed. Being intent on other matters I watched these futile attempts for a time without thinking, unconsciously waiting for him to resume his flight, as one waits for a machine, that has stopped momentarily, to start again without considering the reason of its failure. After perhaps a seventh attempt he slipped from the wooden ledge and fell, fluttering his wings, on to his back on the window sill. The helplessness of his attitude roused me. It flashed upon me that he was in difficulties; he could no longer raise himself; his legs struggled vainly. But, as I stretched out a pencil, meaning to help him to right himself, it came over me that the failure and awkwardness were the approach of death. I laid the pencil down again.

The legs agitated themselves once more. I looked as if for the enemy against which he struggled. I looked out of doors. What had happened there? Presumably it was midday, and work in the fields had stopped. Stillness and quiet had replaced the previous animation. The birds had taken themselves off to feed in the brooks. The horses stood still. Yet the power was there all the same, massed outside indifferent, impersonal, not attending to anything in particular. Somehow it was opposed to the little hay-coloured moth. It was useless to try to do anything. One could only watch the extraordinary efforts made by those tiny legs against an oncoming doom which could, had it chosen, have submerged an entire city, not merely a city, but masses of human beings; nothing, I knew had any chance against death. Nevertheless after a pause of exhaustion the legs fluttered again. It was superb this last protest, and so frantic that he succeeded at last in righting himself. One's sympathies, of course, were all on the side of life. Also, when there was nobody to care or to know, this gigantic effort on the part of an insignificant little moth, against a power of such magnitude, to retain what no one else valued or desired to keep, moved one strangely. Again, somehow, one saw life, a pure bead. I lifted the pencil again, useless though I knew it to be. But even as I did so, the unmistakable tokens of death showed themselves. The body relaxed, and instantly grew stiff. The struggle was over. The insignificant little creature now knew death. As I looked at the dead moth, this minute wayside triumph of so great a force over so mean an antagonist filled me with wonder. Just as life had been strange a few minutes before, so death was now as strange. The moth having righted himself now lay most decently and uncomplainingly composed. O yes, he seemed to say, death is stronger than I am.

# THE COUNTRY OF THE BLIND

## Wolcott Gibbs

Wolcott Gibbs (1902-1958), a New Yorker by birth and preference, worked as a reporter for various newspapers before becoming associated in 1927 with The New Yorker magazine. He served as its drama critic from 1940 until his death and made a brief and ill-advised sortie into motion picture criticism for the magazine in 1944 and 1945.

This essay appeared originally in the Saturday Review of Literature (November 17, 1945) and is reprinted from Season in the Sun and Other Pleasures (1946).

From early December, 1944, until this past September, I was employed to review moving pictures for a magazine of modest but genteel circulation. It was a makeshift arrangement, brought about by the war, and long before the ten months were over, both the editors and I were aware that a mistake had been made. Nothing was actually said, but there was an air of constraint and embarrassment, rather as if we had both made up our minds to ignore the fact that I had suddenly developed a slight impediment in my speech, and when in a moody moment I resigned, everybody was visibly relieved. Since the subscribers gave no indication of either agreeing or disagreeing with anything I wrote, it seemed permissible to deduce that they hadn't bothered to read it. The only comment from the profession appeared in a screen writers' trade-paper on the Coast. It compared me sardonically with Marcel Proust,[1] the idea being that I gave the impression of operating from an insulated cell, in a very fancy atmosphere of anemia and corruption. Since one of my colleagues was described as writing as if his upper plate had worked loose, however, it was possible to regard this as a compliment.

---

[1] Marcel Proust (1871-1922), French novelist known chiefly for the highly complex, minutely detailed picture of French society in his autobiographical novel *A la recherche du temps perdu*, secluded himself in a cork-lined apartment in Paris in order to avoid severe attacks of asthma.

The purpose of this essay is to explain, as clearly as I can and while certain memories are still green, why it seems to me that the cinema resists rational criticism almost as firmly as a six-day bicycle race, or perhaps love. I am conscious of the danger of generalizing too freely from a very brief experience and also of stating some things that are both obvious and highly prejudiced. However, it's a chance I'll have to take, and it is my indignant opinion that ninety percent of the moving pictures exhibited in America are so vulgar, witless, and dull that it is preposterous to write about them in any publication not intended to be read while chewing gum. The exceptions to this indictment are the documentaries, which have, of course, only very limited opportunities to distort life; frank melodramas, which have nothing to do with life and are therefore exempt from criticism; and the occasional pictures, one or two a year at most, which defiantly photograph some recognizable fragment of our common experience and generally lose a good deal of money. They are so few that obviously no one could hope to find regular employment writing about them, and consequently they can be ignored here.

The explanation of the ninety percent is so elementary and it has been offered so many times that it needn't detain us long. The cinema is a medium of entertainment economically feasible only if it can be sold to an audience of probably a hundred million in this country and God knows how many more in the rest of the hemisphere and across the sea. It must, of course, be intelligible to a vast majority of these people. The common level of intelligence in the world is presumably that of the normal adolescent, who has no need or ability to relate the parts to the whole, or the present to the total stretch of time. To him, that is, a baby is a baby, cute and permanent; it has no future and there are no conclusions to be drawn from it. (The persistent survival of Jackie Coogan as a middle-aged man, with a divorce and thinning hair, incidentally, often has an unnerving effect on lady cinema patrons, though they are only vaguely aware of him as a symbol of their own continuity.) The level of formal education, of course, is even lower, so that any system of civilized reference is obviously out of the question. To get in a picture, Homer and Emerson must first be suitably defined, in words of not too many syllables.

The third factor that has to be considered in this universal audience is the manner of life to which it is accustomed; its incredible extremes of wealth and poverty, its varying social concepts, and its differences in language, technical progress, and even climate and clothes. To some extent, Hollywood has succeeded in imposing its own vision of life on the world, so that a cocktail party on Park Avenue need no longer be entirely mysterious to an Eskimo. However, while the cocktail party has gone far beyond life in gaiety and magnificence since people can be taught to accept almost anything visually, it has been necessary to scale it down almost to imbecility in behavior since nobody can be expected to recognize a system of conduct or conversation that has its roots in a more elaborate background than his own. The result of all this is that very little seen or heard on the screen is precisely a picture of anything.

As if these handicaps were not enough, a series of strict, external codes, governing their political and moral content, have been imposed on the films either by organized pressure groups or else by unorganized but highly vocal minorities with a taste for out-size fig leaves. This makes it impracticable to name political philosophies or explain what they stand for, to discuss religion in any terms conceivably startling to the inmates of a parochial school or a Baptist seminary, to speak disparagingly of any specific business, except perhaps dope-running or the white-slave trade, or to deal with sex in any way that might indicate that minor irregularities are not necessarily punishable by a lifetime of social ostracism and a lonely and untended grave. Hollywood, of course, did not frame these rules, but its own earlier excesses of vulgarity (not frankness or daring) were responsible for their existence in the first place, and it has not been noticeably heroic in combating them up to now.

Given all these restrictions, whether imposed by financial considerations or the Hays (now Johnston) Office,[2] it is inevitable that the moving pictures should be just what they are—an astounding parody of life devoted to a society in which anything is physically and materially possible, including perfect happiness, to a race of people who operate intellectually on the level of the New York

---

[2] The Hays Office, first named after its founder, Will Hays, then after his successor, Eric Johnston, censors movies for the trade.

*Daily News,* morally on that of Dayton, Tennessee,[3] and politically
and economically in a total vacuum. I know, of course, that there are
a great many pictures, usually "sophisticated" comedies or glum dramas
of the soil, that *seem* to exceed this definition. It is only an illusion,
however, though often an extremely clever one. Close attention will
inevitably prove that no rules have been broken, that no sinister
worldling ever says anything that would be essentially surprising from
your grandmother, that no doomed share-cropper ever really criticizes
anything more specific than the climate.

How the conscientious reviewer writes about the so-called A
pictures (those that cost more than a million dollars to produce)
is a small but fascinating literary comedy. Aware that he is dealing
with names that are household words from Newark to Bangkok, with
minds that command up to five thousand dollars a week for their
power and agility, and with budgets that rival the national debt,
he gets an uneasy feeling that such massive vulgarity somehow requires massive treatment, though those are not perhaps quite the
words he'd use. Pictures are good or bad to him, for he has his
standards, but their quality, whatever it is, is on the grand scale, and
his discussion of it takes on a very peculiar accent, enormous, educated, and fuzzy. He writes, you might say, rather the way Henry
Wadsworth Longfellow used to look.

Generally speaking, however, he has space for only five or six
hundred words and very little time to put them down. The result
is that he has developed a very special vocabulary in which words
come to transcend their exact and customary meanings—in which,
in a sense, they are detached from the language and inflated like little
balloons, and presently sent spinning, lovely, iridescent, and meaningless, into the wild, blue heaven of critical prose. "Luminous" is such
a word. Coming from the typewriter of a skilful operator, it means
that the performance given by a young woman who has probably
gone through each scene from ten to twenty times with her director
and still has only the vaguest idea what it is all about is strong,
beautiful, humorous, tragic, and lit with something of the same
strange, devouring flame that once burned bright in Duse and Bernhardt. It means, that is, everything and nothing; it is both the non-

---

[3] See footnote 2 to the essay "A Sentimental Journey."

word and the all-word. "Taut" is another and says, in reference to an actor's work, that he is somewhat greater than Booth or Salvini,[4] and, in reference to a story, that it is high time for *Hamlet* to move over. There are a great many of these wonderful words—"haunting," "lyric," "brave," "tender," "compassionate," and, above all, "poignant" occur to me in passing—and they are invaluable in imparting such a cosmic air to a conversation that it is never quite apparent just what precisely is being discussed. The only trouble with all this, in fact, is that, habitually so used, these words can no longer be employed in their original and limited sense, and this is too bad because some of them were rather nice words in the beginning.

The reviewer is also remarkably talented in summarizing the complicated but fundamentally non-existent plots that come his way. These, too, he inflates to several times their natural size, colors with vague but impressive suggestions of other meanings than those that appear on the surface, and also sets adrift in space. In speaking, for instance, of a tornado that has apparently only a simple, melodramatic intent, he is apt to write, "There is, it seems to me, a profound and urgent ["urgent," by the way, is another favorite all-word] symbolism in the storm that carries away Miller's house and drowns his bed-ridden aunt." The symbolism is very seldom explained, but it is apt to delude everybody, including the writer, into believing that a subtle analogy has been offered, unerringly detected, and stylishly exposed.

In addition to complimenting the players and magnifying the plot, it is, of course, the reviewer's duty to go into the difficult matters of direction and photography. The first of these, since the mass mating of minds in any Hollywood picture makes it practically impossible for the layman to tell who did what, is usually conveniently dismissed by the use of a few all-words, or of phrases like "Mr. Desmond displayed great resource in his handling of nuclear mass," or "Mr. Drear's use of causal overtones is provocative, to say the least," both of which I presume mean something or other, though not to me.

Photography, on the other hand, is something actually visible

---

[4] World-renowned actors and actresses: Eleonora Duse (1859-1924), Italian tragedienne; Sarah Bernhardt (1845-1923), French actress and theater-manager; Edwin Booth (1833-1893), American actor; Tommaso Salvini (1829-1915), Italian tragic actor.

on the screen and it is a good deal harder to brush off since the writer is confronted with an insanely complicated, endlessly refined, and wickedly deceptive technical process about which it is reasonable to assume that he knows about as much as he does about the inner workings of a seismograph. He has picked up a few useful terms like "lap dissolve" and "pan take," but for the most part he is obliged to rely on his personal artistic judgment, which, logically enough, since he is not an art critic, is apt to be unformed. He is a great one for "correct" or "striking" compositions, those, that is, that most closely resemble the paintings on sale in department stores, and he is a perennial sucker for the studiously telling details—a dead and falling leaf, a face in a crowd, a hand slowly relaxed—that are all part of a sort of primitive emotional shorthand used by the films to trap the unwary. Since photography is the one thing that Hollywood handles with invariable competence, and often with considerable taste and ingenuity, it seems too bad that the reviewers are neither mechanically nor esthetically equipped to deal with it adequately.

All that I have written, of course, has probably passed through the mind of anyone who has given any appreciable thought to the cinema. It took me ten months of notable physical discomfort and mental confusion, however, before I really saw, in the terms set down here, the whole absurdity of what I was trying to do—to write, that is, for the information of my friends about something that was plainly designed for the entertainment of their cooks—and before I realized that I had no intention of ever doing it again. I once knew an educated and almost excessively cultivated man who really enjoyed reviewing the movies. He was, however, a special case, in that he was unfailingly amused in his wintry way by sex in what he was pleased to call its "contactual aspects," and the idea of an art form fundamentally based on the slow, relentless approach and final passionate collision of two enormous faces struck him as convulsing. He wrote about it all with a wonderful, maidenly distaste, and to the total bewilderment of the motion-picture industry, but he really had the time of his life. He was also a very valuable critic since, free from the terrible spell of Love, he saw a good deal that escaped his earnest colleagues.

# SOME THOUGHTS ON THE COMMON TOAD

## George Orwell

George Orwell (1903-1950), born in Motihari, Bengal, of an Anglo-Indian family, held various jobs in Burma, France, and England and fought against the fascist forces in the Spanish Civil War. Acutely aware of poverty from his own experiences, he was leftist in politics yet distrustful of politicians, whom he satirized in Animal Farm (1945) and Nineteen Eighty-four (1949), a grim prophecy of totalitarianism. The last fifteen years of his life he spent on his farm outside London, a city, he once said, he "detests."

This essay appeared originally in The Tribune (April 12, 1946) and is reprinted from Shooting an Elephant and Other Essays (1950).

Before the swallow, before the daffodil, and not much later than the snowdrop, the common toad salutes the coming of spring after his own fashion, which is to emerge from a hole in the ground, where he has lain buried since the previous autumn, and crawl as rapidly as possible towards the nearest suitable patch of water. Something— some kind of shudder in the earth, or perhaps merely a rise of a few degrees in the temperature—has told him that it is time to wake up: though a few toads appear to sleep the clock round and miss out a year from time to time—at any rate, I have more than once dug them up, alive and apparently well, in the middle of the summer.

At this period, after his long fast, the toad has a very spiritual look, like a strict Anglo-Catholic towards the end of Lent. His movements are languid but purposeful, his body is shrunken, and by contrast his eyes look abnormally large. This allows one to notice, what one might not at another time, that a toad has about the most beautiful eye of any living creature. It is like gold, or more exactly it is like the golden-colored semi-precious stone which one sometimes sees in signet rings, and which I think is called a chrysoberyl.

For a few days after getting into the water the toad concentrates on building up his strength by eating small insects. Presently he has swollen to his normal size again, and then he goes through a phase of intense sexiness. All he knows, at least if he is a male toad, is that he wants to get his arms round something, and if you offer him a stick, or even your finger, he will cling to it with surprising strength and take a long time to discover that it is not a female toad. Frequently one comes upon shapeless masses of ten or twenty toads rolling over and over in the water, one clinging to another without distinction of sex. By degrees, however, they sort themselves out into couples, with the male duly sitting on the female's back. You can now distinguish males from females, because the male is smaller, darker and sits on top, with his arms tightly clasped round the female's neck. After a day or two the spawn is laid in long strings which wind themselves in and out of the reeds and soon become invisible. A few more weeks, and the water is alive with masses of tiny tadpoles which rapidly grow larger, sprout hind-legs, then fore-legs, then shed their tails: and finally, about the middle of the summer, the new generation of toads, smaller than one's thumb-nail but perfect in every particular, crawl out of the water to begin the game anew.

I mention the spawning of the toads because it is one of the phenomena of spring which most deeply appeal to me, and because the toad, unlike the skylark and the primrose, has never had much of a boost from the poets. But I am aware that many people do not like reptiles or amphibians, and I am not suggesting that in order to enjoy the spring you have to take an interest in toads. There are also the crocus, the missel thrush, the cuckoo, the blackthorn, etc. The point is that the pleasures of spring are available to everybody, and cost nothing. Even in the most sordid street the coming of spring will register itself by some sign or other, if it is only a brighter blue between the chimney pots or the vivid green of an elder sprouting on a blitzed site. Indeed it is remarkable how Nature goes on existing unofficially, as it were, in the very heart of London. I have seen a kestrel flying over the Deptford gasworks, and I have heard a first-rate performance by a blackbird in the Euston Road. There must be some hundreds of thousands, if not millions, of birds living inside the four-mile radius,[1] and it is rather a pleasing thought that none of them pays a halfpenny of rent.

As for spring, not even the narrow and gloomy streets round the Bank of England are quite able to exclude it. It comes seeping in everywhere, like one of those new poison gases which pass through all filters. The spring is commonly referred to as "a miracle," and during the past five or six years this worn-out figure of speech has taken on a new lease of life. After the sort of winters we have had to endure recently, the spring does seem miraculous, because it has become gradually harder and harder to believe that it is actually going to happen. Every February since 1940 I have found myself thinking that this time winter is going to be permanent. But Persephone, like the toads, always rises from the dead at about the same moment. Suddenly, towards the end of March, the miracle happens and the decaying slum in which I live is transfigured. Down in the square the sooty privets have turned bright green, the leaves are thickening on the chestnut trees, the daffodils are out, the wallflowers are budding, the policeman's tunic looks positively a pleasant shade of blue, the fishmonger greets his customers with a smile, and even the sparrows are quite a different color, having felt the balminess of the air and nerved themselves to take a bath, their first since last September.

Is it wicked to take a pleasure in spring, and other seasonal changes? To put it more precisely, is it politically reprehensible, while we are all groaning, under the shackles of the capitalist system, to point out that life is frequently more worth living because of a blackbird's song, a yellow elm tree in October, or some other natural phenomenon which does not cost money and does not have what the editors of the Left-wing newspapers call a class angle? There is no doubt that many people think so. I know by experience that a favorable reference to "Nature" in one of my articles is liable to bring me abusive letters, and though the key-word in these letters is usually "sentimental," two ideas seem to be mixed up in them. One is that any pleasure in the actual process of life encourages a sort of political quietism. People, so the thought runs, ought to be discontented, and it is our job to multiply our wants and not simply to increase

---

[1] A zone with a radius of four miles, measured from Charing Cross as the center, beyond which taxi rates rise.

our enjoyment of the things we have already. The other idea is that this is the age of machines and that to dislike the machine, or even to want to limit its domination, is backward-looking, reactionary, and slightly ridiculous. This is often backed up by the statement that a love of Nature is a foible of urbanized people who have no notion what Nature is really like. Those who really have to deal with the soil, so it is argued, do not love the soil, and do not take the faintest interest in birds or flowers, except from a strictly utilitarian point of view. To love the country one must live in the town, merely taking an occasional week-end ramble at the warmer times of year.

This last idea is demonstrably false. Medieval literature, for instance, including the popular ballads, is full of an almost Georgian [2] enthusiasm for Nature, and the art of agricultural peoples such as the Chinese and Japanese centres always round trees, birds, flowers, rivers, mountains. The other idea seems to me to be wrong in a subtler way. Certainly we ought to be discontented, we ought not simply to find out ways of making the best of a bad job, and yet if we kill all pleasure in the actual process of life, what sort of future are we preparing for ourselves? If a man cannot enjoy the return of spring, why should he be happy in a labor-saving Utopia? What will he do with the leisure that the machine will give him? I have always suspected that if our economic and political problems are ever really solved, life will become simpler instead of more complex, and that the sort of pleasure one gets from finding the first primrose will loom larger than the sort of pleasure one gets from eating an ice to the tune of a Wurlitzer. I think that by retaining one's childhood love of such things as trees, fishes, butterflies and—to return to my first instance—toads, one makes a peaceful and decent future a little more probable, and that by preaching the doctrine that nothing is to be admired except steel and concrete, one merely makes it a little surer that human beings will have no outlet for their surplus energy except in hatred and leader-worship.

At any rate, spring is here, even in London, N.1, and they can't stop you enjoying it. This is a satisfying reflection. How many a time have I stood watching the toads mating, or a pair of hares having a boxing match in the young corn, and thought of all the

---

[2] A term for the work of poets of the reign (1910-1936) of George V who cultivated the sensational effects of nature imagery.

important persons who would stop me enjoying this if they could. But luckily they can't. So long as you are not actually ill, hungry, frightened or immured in a prison or a holiday camp, spring is still spring. The atom bombs are piling up in the factories, the police are prowling through the cities, the lies are streaming from the loudspeakers, but the earth is still going round the sun, and neither the dictators nor the bureaucrats, deeply as they disapprove of the process, are able to prevent it.

# OUT OF A BOOK

## Elizabeth Bowen

Elizabeth Bowen was born in 1899 in Dublin, Ireland, of Anglo-Irish ancestry and spent her early childhood on the family estate, Bowen's Court, Kildorrery, County Cork. At the age of seven, her family moved to southern England where she remained until, at nineteen, she went to London. Here she began writing the many novels and short stories that have established her reputation for precision and beauty of style and for remarkable evocations of childhood experience.

This essay appeared originally in Orion III (1946) and is reprinted from Collected Impressions (1950).

I know that I have in my make-up layers of synthetic experience, and that the most powerful of my memories are only half true. Reduced to the minimum, to the what did happen, my life would be unrecognizable by me. Those layers of fictitious memory densify as they go deeper down. And this surely must be the case with everyone else who reads deeply, ravenously, unthinkingly, sensuously, as a child. The overlapping and haunting of life by fiction began, of course, before there was anything to be got from the printed page; it began from the day one was old enough to be told a story or shown a picture book. It went on up to the age when a bookish attitude towards books began to be inculcated by education. The young person is then thrown out of Eden; for evermore his brain is to stand posted between his self and the story. Appreciation of literature is the end of magic: in place of the virgin susceptibility to what is written he is given taste, something to be refined and trained.

Happily, the Eden, like a natal climate, can be unconsciously remembered, and the magic stored up in those years goes on secreting under to-day's chosen sensations and calculated thoughts. What entered the system during childhood remains; and remains indistinguishable from the life of those years because it was the greater part of the life. Probably children, if they said what they thought, would be much franker about the insufficiency of so-called real life to the requirements of those who demand to be really alive. Nothing but the story can meet the untried nature's need and capacity for the whole. Of course one cannot narrow down children to the reading child; but I could not as a child, and I cannot now, conceive what the non-reading child must be like inside. Outdoor children were incomprehensible to me when I was their age, and I still find them dull; I could not, and cannot, find out what makes them do what they do, or why they like what they like; and of such children now they are grown up I can only say that I cannot conceive what they remember, if they do remember—for how can even the senses carry imprints when there was no story? The non-reading active children were not stupid; they had their senses. Nor was it the clever children who read most, or who were at any rate the ones who inhaled fiction—quite apart there were always the horrible little students, future grown-ups, who pursued knowledge. The light-headed reading child and the outdoor child had more in common (in fact, the life of sensation) than either had with the student. Readers of my kind were the heady ones, the sensationalists—recognizing one another at sight we were banded together inside a climate of our own. Landscapes or insides of houses or streets or gardens, outings or even fatigue duties all took the cast of the book we were circulating at the time; and the reading made of us an electric ring. Books were story or story-poetry books: we were unaware that there could be any others.

Some of the heady group remained wonderfully proof against education: having never graduated these are the disreputable grownups who snap up shiny magazines and garner and carry home from libraries fiction that the critics ignore. They read as we all once read—because they must: without fiction, either life would be insufficient or the winds from the north would blow too cold. They read as we all read when we were twelve; but unfortunately the magic has been adulterated; the dependence has become ignominious —it becomes an enormity, inside the full-sized body, to read without the brain. Now the stories they seek go on being children's stories, only with sex added to the formula; and somehow the addition queers everything. These readers, all the same, are the great malleable bulk, the majority, the greater public—hence best-sellers, with their partly artful, partly unconscious play on a magic that has gone stale. The only above-board grown-up children's stories are detective stories.

No, it is not only our fate but our business to lose innocence, and once we have lost that it is futile to attempt a picnic in Eden. One kind of power to read, or power that reading had over us, is gone. And not only that: it is a mistake to as much as re-open the books of childhood—they are bare ruined choirs. Everything has evaporated from those words, leaving them meaningless on the page. This is the case, for me, even with Dickens—I cannot read him now because I read him exhaustively as a child. Though I did not in those years read all his books, I cannot now read any that I did not read then—there is no more oxygen left, for me, anywhere in the atmosphere of his writing. The boredom I seem to feel as I pursue the plots is, really, a flagging of my intellect in this (by me) forever used up and devitalized air. I came to an end with Dickens when I had absorbed him into myself.

Yes, one stripped bare the books of one's childhood to make oneself—it is inevitable that there should be nothing left when one goes back to them. The fickleness of children and very young persons shocks their elders—children abandon people, for instance, without a flicker, with a simplicity that really ought not to be hurting: the abandoned one has been either a "best" friend or an object of hero-worship, and the more emotionally fruitful and fanciful the relationship, the more complete the break. "Where is So-and-so these days? I don't seem to have heard anything about him (or her) for a long time. Haven't you two got any more plans?"—"Oh, I can't be bothered." What applies to people applies to books, and for the same reason: everything that was wanted has been taken; only the husk or, still worse, mortifying repetition remains. The child is on the make—rapacious, mobile and single-minded. If the exhausted book survives physical abandonment—being given away or left out in the garden in the rain—it languishes on in its owner's indifferent keeping; however, once memory and sentiment have had time to set in and gather about it, it is safe. I still keep a row of books I loved as a child—but I neither wish nor dare to touch them.

What do I mean by those books making myself? In the first

place, they were power-testing athletics for my imagination—cross-country runs into strange country, sprints, long and high jumps. It was exhilarating to discover what one could feel: the discovery itself was an advance. Then, by successively "being" a character in every book I read, I doubled the meaning of everything that happened in my otherwise constricted life. Books introduced me to, and magnified, desire and danger. They represented life, with a conclusiveness I had no reason to challenge, as an affair of mysteries and attractions, in which each object or place or face was in itself a volume of promises and deceptions, and in which nothing was impossible. Books made me see everything that I saw either as a symbol or as having its place in a mythology—in fact, reading gave bias to my observations of everything in the between-times when I was not reading. And obviously, the characters in the books gave prototypes under which, for evermore, to assemble all living people. This did not by any means simplify people for me; it had the reverse effect, and I was glad that it should—the characters who came out of my childish reading to obsess me were the incalculable ones, who always moved in a blur of potentialities. It appeared that nobody who mattered was capable of being explained. Thus was inculcated a feeling for the dark horse. I can trace in all people whom I have loved a succession from book characters—not from one only, from a fusion of many. "Millions of strange shadows on you tend." [1]

Also the expectation, the search, was geographic. I was and I am still on the look out for places where something happened: the quivering needle swings in turn to a prospect of country, a town unwrapping itself from folds of landscape or seen across water, or a significant house. Such places are haunted—scenes of acute sensation for someone, vicariously me. My identity, so far as I can pin it down at all, resides among these implacable likes or dislikes, these subjections to magnetism spaced out between ever-widening lacunae of indifference. I feel certain that if I *could* read my way back, analytically, through the books of my childhood, the clues to everything could be found.

The child lives in the book; but just as much the book lives in the child. I mean that, admittedly, the process of reading is recip-

---

[1] Shakespeare, Sonnet 53.

rocal; the book is no more than a formula, to be furnished out with images out of the reader's mind. At any age, the reader must come across: the child reader is the most eager and quick to do so; he not only lends to the story, he flings into the story the whole of his sensuous experience which from being limited is the more intense. Book dishes draw saliva to the mouth; book fears raise gooseflesh and make the palms clammy; book suspense make the cheeks burn and the heart thump. Still more, at the very touch of a phrase there is a surge of brilliant visual images: the child rushes up the scenery for the story. When the story, as so often happens, demands what has not yet come into stock, indefatigable makeshifts are arrived at— as when a play that calls for elaborate staging is performed by an enterprising little company with scanty equipment and few drop-scenes. Extension (to draw an iceberg out of a fishmonger's ice-block) or multiplication (to make a thin, known wood into a track-less forest) goes on. For castles, gorges, or anything else spectacular out of art or nature, recollections of picture postcards, posters or travel albums are drawn on; and, of course, the child to-day has amassed a whole further scenic stock from the cinema. This provision of a convincing *where* for the story is a reflex.

For the child, any real-life scene that has once been sucked into the ambience of the story is affected, or infected, forever. The road, cross-roads, corner of a wood, cliff, flight of steps, town square, quayside or door in a wall keeps a transmuted existence: it has not only given body to fiction, it has partaken of fiction's body. Such a thing, place or scene cannot again be walked past indifferently; it exerts a pull and sets up a tremor; and it is to indent the memory for life. It is at these points, indeed, that what I have called synthetic experience has its sources. Into that experience come relationships, involving valid emotion, between the child reader and book characters; a residuum of the book will be in all other emotions that are to follow.

In reverse, there are the real-life places—towns, seaports, suburbs of London—unknown to the child, though heard of, which become "real" through being also in books. For instance, after *David Copperfield* I could not hear either Dover or Yarmouth mentioned, in the most ordinary context, without excitement: I had a line on them. Towns that were in books, and the routes between them travelled by

characters, stood out in relief on the neutral map of England. Not a
Londoner, I was continuously filling in and starring my map of the
environs—at Richmond lived Sir Percy, the Scarlet Pimpernel,[2] and
his wife Marguerite, who fainted into a bed of heliotrope in her
riverside garden; at Highgate, the Steerforths and Rosa Dartle;[3] at
Blackheath and Lewisham, the E. Nesbit children.[4] When I came to
read *Kipps*,[5] I was made dizzy by the discovery that I had, for years,
been living in two places, Hythe and Folkestone, that were in a
book. Historic places one was taken to see meant no more and no
less to me than this; history was fiction—it took me a long time to be
able to see that it gained anything further from being "true."

Though not all reading children grow up to be writers, I take
it that most creative writers must in their day have been reading
children. All through creative writing there must run a sense of
dishonesty and of debt. In fact, is there such a thing, any more, as
creative writing? The imagination, which may appear to bear such
individual fruit, is rooted in a compost of forgotten books. The
apparent choices of art are nothing but addictions, pre-dispositions:
where did these come from, how were they formed? The aesthetic
is nothing but a return to images that will allow nothing to take
their place; the aesthetic is nothing but an attempt to disguise and
glorify the enforced return. All susceptibility belongs to the age of
magic, the Eden where fact and fiction were the same; the imaginative writer was the imaginative child, who relied for life upon being
lied to—and how, now, is he to separate the lies from his consciousness of life? If he be a novelist, all his psychology is merely a new
parade of the old mythology. We have relied on our childhoods, on
the sensations of childhood, because we mistake vividness for purity;
actually, the story was there first—one is forced to see that it was the
story that apparelled everything in celestial light. It could lead to
madness to look back and back for the true primary impression or
sensation; those we did ever experience we have forgotten—we only
remember that to which something was added. Almost no experi-

---

[2] The chief character of Baroness Orczy's historical romance of the French Revolution, *The Scarlet Pimpernel* (1905).
[3] Characters in Charles Dickens' *David Copperfield* (1849-50).
[4] Edith Nesbit Bland (1858-1924), under the pen name "E. Nesbit," wrote
stories of and for children.
[5] A novel (1905) by H. G. Wells.

ence, however much simplified by the distance of time, is to be vouched for as being wholly my own—*did* I live through that, or was I told that it happened, or did I read it? When I write, I am re-creating what was created for me. The gladness of vision, in writing, is my own gladness, but not at my own vision. I may see, for instance, a road running uphill, a skyline, a figure coming slowly over the hill—the approach of the figure is momentous, accompanied by fear or rapture or fear of rapture or a rapture of fear. But who and how is this? Am I sure this is not a figure out of a book?

# THE MEANING OF TREASON

## *Rebecca West*

*Rebecca West was born in 1892 in County Kerry, Ireland. After a short time on the stage, she turned to writing on politics and woman suffrage for London newspapers. She is the author of several novels, but her most conspicuous recent successes have been in Black Lamb and Grey Falcon (1941), a study of Yugoslavia, and in The Meaning of Treason (1947), her thoughtful report of the treason trials following the defeat of Germany in World War II.*

*This essay is reprinted as it appeared originally in Harper's Magazine (October 1947). In an abbreviated and slightly altered form it became the "Epilogue" to The Meaning of Treason.*

From time to time during my career as a journalist I have reported notable law cases, and I know that it is not only morbidity which makes the public enjoy following the trial of a serious crime. It is very difficult for those who study life to find a story that comes to its end under their eyes. When we select an individual whose course we want to trace, it is as likely as not that he covers his tracks with secrecy, or moves to a field outside our view, or delays his end until we ourselves have ended. That is why classical history is a valuable study; we can see the whole story, the beginning, the middle, and the end of Greece and Rome, Egypt and Persia. That is why the lives of great men in the past teach us more than knowledge of great men in the present; we know their remoter consequences. The dock brings a like illumination.

Here an individual story comes to its end in a collision with the community. Every case has its unique intellectual and spiritual significance. The appearance of the accused person, the changes in his face and voice, his agreement with society as disclosed by the witnesses who approve of him, his conflict with society as disclosed by the witnesses who disapprove of him, his relation to the crime of which he is truly or falsely accused, always reveal a special case. But the crime which he committed, if he was justly accused, or the other crime which was committed by the representatives of society if he was falsely accused, has always the same cause: refusal to respect the individuality of another or others. A world in which each man respected the soul of all other men, no matter how little they seemed to merit respect, would be crimeless.

There is an obvious political implication to be drawn from this. The authoritarian state is *ipso facto* criminal. When I covered the trial of William Joyce ("Lord Haw-Haw")[1] for the *New Yorker* I saw a man in the dock who was doubly criminal. He had committed crimes against the law out of his desire to substitute a criminal state for a state which, if not completely innocent, aimed at the innocence of freedom. It was obviously doubtful if he would ever have been guilty of any offense had he not been tainted by this political guilt. But when his actual offense against the law was examined it was seen that he had acted in a manner which had long been extolled by many who were in theory pure of that guilt and firmly opposed to the authoritarian state.

Almost all contemporary left-wing writers of this generation and the last attacked the idea of nationalism. It was true that many of these attacks were made under the delusion that the words nationalism and imperialism mean the same thing, whereas nationalism—which means simply a special devotion of a people to its own material and spiritual achievements—implies no desire for the annexation of other territories and enslavement of other peoples. But a great many of these attacks were made under no such apprehension. It was genuinely felt that it was pure superstition which required a man to feel any warmer emotion about his own land, race, and people than about any other. Why then should any man feel a lump in his throat when he saw his flag or the statue at the harbor gate of his native

---

[1] William Joyce (1906-1946), under the name "Lord Haw-Haw," broadcast anti-British propaganda from Berlin during World War II; he came up for trial for treason in 1945. Evidence produced in the trial showed that though Joyce regarded himself as "pure British," he had been born in Brooklyn and that his British father had become, before his son's birth, a naturalized American citizen. In her book, Miss West explains that Joyce, having moved with his family to Ireland, found there, under the rule of England, a police state which inspired his early interest in fascism.

land, or feel that in a dispute between his people and another he must obey the will of his kin and not aid their enemy?

I watched the trial of William Joyce, and of all traitors who were charged in courts which I could conveniently attend. They had all cleared their throats of that lump, they had all made that transit of frontiers recommended by the rationalists; and this had landed them in the service of the persecutors of reason, the fanatical believers in frontiers as the demarcation lines between the saved and the damned. But as their lives were unfolded it appeared that none of them had cast off their nationalist prejudice because of their strength, but had been divested of it by maladjusted ambition, by madness, by cowardice, by weakness. It seemed as if contemporary rationalists had been wrong, and I remembered that the trouble about man is twofold. He cannot learn truths which are too complicated; he forgets truths which are too simple. After I had seen twenty traitors tried it seemed to me that the reason why they were in the dock, why intellectuals preach against nationalism, is that we have forgotten certain simple truths.

We have forgotten that we live outward from the center of a circle and that what is nearest to the center is most real to us. If a man cut his hand, it hurts him more than if he cut some other man's hand; therefore he is more careful to guard his own. Even if he spend his whole life in teaching himself that we are all of one body, and that therefore his neighbor's pain is his also, he will still suffer more when his own hand is hurt, for the message then runs straight from his palm and fingers to his brain, traveling at a speed faster than light or sound, which bear the news of others' accidents. Throughout his life it remains true that what is nearest to his body is of greatest interest to his mind. When a baby is given food and held warmly by a certain woman, he grows up to feel a closer concern for her than for other women of her generation, and at her death will feel greatly disturbed. Should he be institution-bred and have no woman as his particular slave and tyrant, grievance will sour him till his last day.

If in his maturity he should live with a woman for any considerable period of time, he and she are apt, unless they are overtaken by certain obviously disagreeable circumstances, to behave as though there were a complete community of interest between them. There must have been some instinctive liking between them or they would never have been drawn together in the first place; they became involved in each other's prosperity; experience has taught each how the other will behave in most eventualities. Therefore they do better by one another than strangers would. Should he have children by this or any other woman, they will have great power over him, while other children will have little or none. He will know so much more about them. The veiled moment of their conception is his secret, and resemblances to him, to a familiar woman, or to his kin enable him to trace their inner lives, disguised though they be first by their inarticulateness and then by their articulateness. He can read them by the light of his own nature, and read his own nature by their light, and will have a sense of fusion between himself and those who are so inextricably tangled with that self.

If that man live in a house during the days of his childhood, he will know it better than any house he lives in later, though it shelter him forty years longer; and though the staircase wind as deviously as any in the world he will find his way down it in the darkness as surely as if it were straight. All his life long, when he hears talk of woods, he shall see beechwoods, if he come from a Buckinghamshire village, and a castle to him shall stand on Castle Rock, if Edinburgh was his home; and in the one case he shall know Southern English country folk, and in the other Lowland Scottish townsfolk, better than other Britons. Born and bred in England, he will find it easier to understand the English than the rest of men, not for any mystical reason, but because their language is his, because he is fully acquainted with their customs, and because he is the product of their common history. So also each continent enjoys a vague unity of self-comprehension, and is divided from the others by a sharp disunity; and even those who profess the closest familiarity with the next world speak with more robust certainty of this world and seem not to want to leave it.

This is not to say that a man loves what is nearest to him. He may hate his parents, his wife, and his children. Millions have done so. On the tables of the Law it was written "Honor thy father and thy mother, as the Lord God hath commanded thee; that thy days may be prolonged, and that it may go well with thee in the land which the Lord thy God giveth thee," [2] and it is advice of almost gross practicality aimed at preventing the faithful from abandoning themselves to their natural impulses and wasting all their force on family rows. St. Paul, that great artist who perpetually betrayed his art because he was also a great man of action, and constantly abandoned the search for truth to seek instead a myth to inspire vigorous action, tried to gild the bondage of man to the familiar. "So ought men to love their own wives as their own body," he says. "He that loveth his wife loveth himself. For no man ever yet hated his own flesh, but nourisheth it and cherisheth it, even as the Lord the Church." [3] But countless men have hated their own flesh. Everywhere and at all times men have carried such hatred to the point of slaying it, and still more have persecuted it by abstinence and mortification and debauchery. It has a value to them far above their loathing or their liking. It is their own flesh and they can have no direct experience of any other. Not with all the gold in the world or by incessant prayer can we obtain another instrument-case, packed with these our only instruments, the five senses, by which alone we can irradiate the universe that is a black void around us, and build a small irradiated platform in that darkness. A wife is someone who has stood on that irradiated platform long enough to be fully examined and to add the testimony of her own senses as to the nature of that encircling mystery. She may be loved or hated, or loved and hated, and serve in that research.

A child knows that what is near is easier for him to handle than what is far. All men took it for granted till recent times, when it was challenged, together with some other traditional assumptions, not because they had proved unsound, but because a number of urbanized populations from which the intellectual classes were largely drawn had lost their sense of spiritual as well as material process. They had lost their sense of material process owing to the development of the machine; goods which had formerly been produced by simple and comprehensible processes, often carried on where they could be witnessed by the consumer, were now produced by elaborate processes, not to be grasped by people without mechanical training, and carried on in the privacy of the large factories.

---

[2] Deuteronomy 5:16.
[3] See Ephesians 5:28-29.

The reason for their ignorance of spiritual process was the urban lack of the long memory and the omniscient gossip enjoyed by the village. The townsman is surrounded by people whose circumstances he does not know and whose heredities are the secrets of other districts; and he is apt to take their dissimulating faces and their clothed bodies as the sum of them. People began to think of each other in a new way; as simple with a simplicity in fact unknown in organic life. They ignored the metabolism of human nature, by which experiences are absorbed into the mind and magically converted into personality, which rejects much of the material life brings to it and handles the rest to serve the interests of love or hate, good or evil, life or death, according to an inhabiting daemon, whose reasons are never given. Man conceived himself as living reasonably under the instruction of the five senses, which tell him to seek pleasure and avoid pain.

The first effect of this rational conception of life was cheerful vulgarity; and there are worse things than that. Man might well have felt this view of his destiny as a relief after the Christian philosophy, which abased his origin to criminality, and started him so low only to elevate him to the height, most disagreeable to most people, of company with godhead, after dragging him through all sorts of unpalatable experiences, including participation in a violent and apparently unnecessary death. In so far as a man adopted the new and rationalist philosophy he could be compared to an actor who, after spending a lifetime playing Hamlet and Othello and King Lear, retires to keep a country pub. All was thenceforward to go at a peaceable jog-trot. Children were to grow up straight striplings of light, undeformed by repression, unscarred by conflicts, because their parents would hand them over in their earliest years to the care of pedagogic experts. Divorce was not to be reckoned as a disgrace nor as a tragedy nor even as a failure, but as a pleasurable extension of experience, like travel. Furthermore—and this was considered as the sanest adjustment of all—the ardors of patriotism were to be abandoned, and replaced by a cool resolution to place one's country on a level with all others in one's affections, and to hand it over without concern to the dominion of any other power which could offer it greater material benefits. It was not out of cynicism that the benefits demanded were material: it was believed that the material automatically produced the intellectual and the spiritual. These reasonable steps having been taken, there was to follow harmony. The only peril was that it might become too sweet.

But the five senses had evidently not been rightly understood. Such children as were surrendered by their parents to expert treatment, complained against that surrender as if it had been any other kind of abandonment. They quarreled with the pedagogues as much as they would have quarreled with their parents; but, the bond of the flesh being absent, there was something sapless in their quarrels, and there was less energy engendered. Sexual life was not noticeably smoother than it had been. The epic love of marriage and the lyric love-song of the encounter both lost much by the pretense that they were the same. Nor, as patriotism was discredited, did peace come nearer. Indeed, the certainty of war now arched over the earth like a second sky, inimical to the first. If harmony had been our peril, we were preserved from it, both within and without. For it was plain that, as Christian philosophy had so harshly averred, the world was a stage on which an extraordinary drama, not yet fully comprehended by the intellect, was being performed; and its action was now an agony. But, owing to the adoption of the rationalist philosophy, some of the actors filling the most important parts were now incapable of speaking their lines. It appeared that *Hamlet* and *Othello* and *King Lear* would be no longer cathartic tragedies but repellent and distressing farces if the leading characters had, in the climactic scenes, been overtaken by the delusion that they had retired and were keeping country pubs.

So the evil moment came and was clear: not surpassed in evil since the days of the barbarian invasions. The devil of nationalism had been driven out of man, but he had not become the headquarters of the dove. Instead there had entered into him the seven devils of internationalism, and he was torn by their frenzies. Then what is against all devils came to his aid. The achievement (which, as yet, is unfinished, since peace does not reign) was accomplished by a continuance of the drama in spite of the difficulties created by the rationalist philosophy. Since the actors cast to play the leading parts would not speak, the action was carried on by the peoples who used to walk to and fro at the back of the scene, softly laughing or softly weeping, or simply quietly being. Now these people streamed across the continents, inscribing their beliefs on the surface of the earth by the course of their flights, and on the sites of their martyrdoms. They defeated fascism by not being fascist. They showed the contrast between fascism and nonfascism so clearly that the world, wishing to live, defended their side because it could be seen that they were the representatives of life. As they exorcised the devils from the body of Europe they seemed to affirm certain values. It was perhaps true that the origin of man was in criminality, for once a community refused to make the effort of seeking the company of godhead it certainly became criminal. It was perhaps true that hedonism is an impotent gospel, for now it could be seen that pleasure means nothing to many men. As fast as those who ran to save their lives ran those who ran to slay them, even if their pursuit, pressed too hard, might change them into fugitives, whose own lives were in danger. Now the scorned bonds of the flesh asserted their validity. It was the final and unbearable misery of these flights that husbands were separated from their wives, and parents lost sight of their children. The men who performed the cruelest surgery on these families, who threw the husband and wife into the gas chamber while the children traveled by train to an unknown destination, had themselves been brought up to condemn their own ties of blood. The anguish of the divided was obviously holy. The contentment of those who felt no reluctance to divide was plainly damned.

In this day of exposition those who made the other sacrifice of the near for the far, and preferred other countries to their own, proved also to be unholy. The relationship between a man and a fatherland is always disturbed by conflict, if either man or fatherland is highly developed. A man's demands for liberty must at some point challenge the limitations the state imposes on the individual for the sake of the mass. If he is to carry on the national tradition he must wrestle with those who, speaking in its name, desire to crystallize it at the point reached by the previous generation. In any case national life itself must frequently exasperate him, because it is the medium in which he is expressing himself, and every craftsman or artist is repelled by the resistance of his medium to his will. All men should have a drop or two of treason in their veins, if the nations are not to go soft like so many sleepy bears.

Yet to be a traitor is most miserable. All the men I saw in the prisoner's dock were sad as they stood their trials, not only because they were going to be punished. They would have been sad even if they had never been brought to justice. They had forsaken the familiar medium; they had trusted themselves to the mercies of those who had no reason to care for them; knowing their custodians' indifference they had lived for long in fear; and they were aware that they had thrown away their claim on those who might naturally have felt affection for them. Strangers, as King Solomon put it, were filled with their wealth, and their labors were in the house of a stranger, and they mourned at the last when their flesh and body were consumed.[4] As a divorce sharply recalls what a happy marriage should be, so the treachery of these men recalled what a nation should be; a shelter where all talents are generously recognized, all forgivable oddities forgiven, all viciousness quietly frustrated, and those who lack talent honored for equivalent contributions of graciousness. Each of these men was as dependent on the good opinion of others as one is oneself; they needed a nation which was also a hearth, and their capacity for suffering made it tragic that they had gone out from their own hearth to suffer among strangers, because the intellectual leaders of their time had professed a philosophy which was scarcely more than a lapse of memory, and had forgotten, that a hearth gives out warmth.

based on concentric circles
flames decentralization for treason
partisan viewpoint
respect individuals, but respect oneself
machines, society intellects

Is it bad to
break away

---

[4] See Proverbs 5:10-11.

# THE FUTURE IS NOW

## Katherine Anne Porter

Katherine Anne Porter, born in Texas in 1894, has lived in
New York, Mexico, Europe, and lately in California, and has
been a newspaper reporter, editor, essayist, and translator of
French, Spanish, and Latin-American fiction. Her short
stories began to appear regularly in the 1920's and were first
collected in Flowering Judas (1930); two additional volumes
of short stories and five short novels have also been published.

This essay appeared originally in Mademoiselle (November
1950) and is reprinted from The Days Before (1952).

Not so long ago I was reading in a magazine with an enormous
circulation some instructions as to how to behave if and when we
see that flash brighter than the sun which means that the atom
bomb has arrived. I read of course with the intense interest of one
who has everything to learn on this subject; but at the end, the
advice dwindled to this: the only real safety seems to lie in simply
being somewhere else at the time, the farther away the better; the
next best, failing access to deep shelters, bombproof cellars and all,
is to get under a stout table—that is, just what you might do if
someone were throwing bricks through your window and you were
too nervous to throw them back.

This comic anticlimax to what I had been taking as a serious
educational piece surprised me into real laughter, hearty and carefree.
It is such a relief to be told the truth, or even just the facts, so
pleasant not to be coddled with unreasonable hopes. That very
evening I was drawn away from my work table to my fifth-story
window by one of those shrill terror-screaming sirens which our
excitement-loving city government used then to affect for so many
occasions: A fire? Police chasing a gangster? Somebody being got
to the hospital in a hurry? Some distinguished public guest being

94

transferred from one point to another? Strange aircraft coming over, maybe? Under the lights of the corner crossing of the great avenue, a huge closed vehicle whizzed past, screaming. I never knew what it was, had not in fact expected to know; no one I could possibly ask would know. Now that we have bells clamoring away instead for such events, we all have one doubt less, if perhaps one expectancy more. The single siren's voice means to tell us only one thing.

But at that doubtful moment, framed in a lighted window level with mine in the apartment house across the street, I saw a young man in a white T-shirt and white shorts at work polishing a long, beautiful dark table top. It was obviously his own table in his own flat, and he was enjoying his occupation. He was bent over in perfect concentration, rubbing, sandpapering, running the flat of his palm over the surface, standing back now and then to get the sheen of light on the fine wood. I am sure he had not even raised his head at the noise of the siren, much less had he come to the window. I stood there admiring his workmanlike devotion to a good job worth doing, and there flashed through me one of those pure fallacies of feeling which suddenly overleap reason: surely all that effort and energy so irreproachably employed were not going to be wasted on a table that was to be used merely for crawling under at some unspecified date. Then why take all those pains to make it beautiful? Any sort of old board would do.

I was so shocked at this treachery of the lurking Foul Fiend (despair *is* a foul fiend, and this was despair) I stood a moment longer, looking out and around, trying to collect my feelings, trying to think a little. Two windows away and a floor down in the house across the street, a young woman was lolling in a deep chair, reading and eating fruit from a little basket. On the sidewalk, a boy and a girl dressed alike in checkerboard cotton shirts and skin-tight blue denims, a costume which displayed acutely the structural differences of their shapes, strolled along with their arms around each other. I believe this custom of lovers walking enwreathed in public was imported by our soldiers of the First World War from France, from Paris indeed. "You didn't see that sort of thing here before," certain members of the older generation were heard to remark quite often, in a tone of voice. Well, one sees quite a lot of it now, and it is a very pretty, reassuring sight. Other citizens of all sizes and kinds and ages were crossing back and forth; lights flashed red and green, punctually. Motors zoomed by, and over the great city—but where am I going? I never read other peoples' descriptions of great cities, more particularly if it is a great city I know. It doesn't belong here anyway, except that I had again that quieting sense of the continuity of human experience on this earth, its perpetual aspirations, setbacks, failures and re-beginnings in eternal hope; and that, with some appreciable differences of dress, customs and means of conveyance, so people have lived and moved in the cities they have built for more millennia than we are yet able to account for, and will no doubt build and live for as many more.

Why did this console me? I cannot say; my mind is of the sort that can often be soothed with large generalities of that nature. The silence of the spaces between the stars does not affright me, as it did Pascal,[1] because I am unable to imagine it except poetically; and my awe is not for the silence and space of the endless universe but for the inspired imagination of man, who can think and feel so, and turn a phrase like that to communicate it to us. Then too, I like the kind of honesty and directness of the young soldier who lately answered someone who asked him if he knew what he was fighting for. "I sure do," he said, "I am fighting to live." And as for the future, I was once reading the first writings of a young girl, an apprentice author, who was quite impatient to get on with the business and find her way into print. There is very little one can say of use in such matters, but I advised her against haste—she could so easily regret it. "Give yourself time," I said, "the future will take care of itself." This opinionated young person looked down her little nose at me and said, "The future is now." She may have heard the phrase somewhere and liked it, or she may just have naturally belonged to that school of metaphysics; I am sure she was too young to have investigated the thought deeply. But maybe she was right and the future does arrive every day and it is all we have, from one second to the next.

So I glanced again at the young man at work, a proper-looking candidate for the armed services, and realized the plain, homely fact: he was not preparing a possible shelter, something to cower

---

[1] Blaise Pascal (1623-1662), French philosopher, expressed this fright in his *Pensées*, III.206.

under trembling; he was restoring a beautiful surface to put his books and papers on, to serve his plates from, to hold his cocktail tray and his lamp. He was full of the deep, right, instinctive, human belief that he and the table were going to be around together for a long time. Even if he is off to the army next week, it will be there when he gets back. At the very least, he is doing something he feels is worth doing now, and that is no small thing.

At once the difficulty, and the hope, of our special time in this world of Western Europe and America is that we have been brought up for many generations in the belief, however tacit, that all humanity was almost unanimously engaged in going forward, naturally to better things and to higher reaches. Since the eighteenth century at least when the Encyclopedists seized upon the Platonic theory that the highest pleasure of mankind was pursuit of the good, the true, and the beautiful, progress, in precisely the sense of perpetual, gradual amelioration of the hard human lot, has been taught popularly not just as theory of possibility but as an article of faith and the groundwork of a whole political doctrine. Mr. Toynbee has even simplified this view for us with picture diagrams of various sections of humanity, each in its own cycle rising to its own height, struggling beautifully on from craggy level to level, but always upward.[2] Whole peoples are arrested at certain points, and perish there, but others go on. There is also the school of thought, Oriental and very ancient, which gives to life the spiral shape, and the spiral moves by nature upward. Even adherents of the circular or recurring-cycle school, also ancient and honorable, somehow do finally allow that the circle is a thread that spins itself out one layer above another, so that even though it is perpetually at every moment passing over a place it has been before, yet by its own width it will have risen just so much higher.

These are admirable attempts to get a little meaning and order into our view of our destiny, in that same spirit which moves the artist to labor with his little handful of chaos, bringing it to co-

[2] Arnold J. Toynbee (1889-    ), English historian whose *Study of History* (11 vols., 1934-1959) is based on a cyclical principle of "challenge and response." Diagrams of the theory were published in *Life* magazine (February 23, 1948, pp. 118-124).

herency within a frame; but on the visible evidence we must admit that in human nature the spirit of contradiction more than holds its own. Mankind has always built a little more than he has hitherto been able or willing to destroy; got more children than he has been able to kill; invented more laws and customs than he had any intention of observing; founded more religions than he was able to practice or even to believe in; made in general many more promises than he could keep; and has been known more than once to commit suicide through mere fear of death. Now in our time, in his pride to explore his universe to its unimaginable limits and to exceed his possible powers, he has at last produced an embarrassing series of engines too powerful for their containers and too tricky for their mechanicians; millions of labor-saving gadgets which can be rendered totally useless by the mere failure of the public power plants, and has reduced himself to such helplessness that a dozen or less of the enemy could disable a whole city by throwing a few switches. This paradoxical creature has committed all these extravagances and created all these dangers and sufferings in a quest—we are told—for peace and security.

How much of this are we to believe, when with the pride of Lucifer, the recklessness of Icarus, the boldness of Prometheus and the intellectual curiosity of Adam and Eve (yes, intellectual; the serpent promised them wisdom if . . .) man has obviously outreached himself, to the point where he cannot understand his own science or control his own inventions. Indeed he has become as the gods, who have over and over again suffered defeat and downfall at the hands of their creatures. Having devised the most exquisite and instantaneous means of communication to all corners of the earth, for years upon years friends were unable even to get a postcard message to each other across national frontiers. The newspapers assure us that from the kitchen tap there flows a chemical, cheap and available, to make a bomb more disturbing to the imagination even than the one we so appallingly have; yet no machine has been invented to purify that water so that it will not spoil even the best tea or coffee. Or at any rate, it is not in use. We are the proud possessors of rocket bombs that go higher and farther and faster than any ever before, and there is some talk of a rocket ship shortly to take off for the moon. (My plan is to stow away.) We may indeed reach the moon some day, and I dare predict that will happen before we have devised a decent system of city garbage disposal.

This lunatic atom bomb has succeeded in rousing the people of all nations to the highest point of unanimous moral dudgeon; great numbers of persons are frightened who never really had much cause to be frightened before. This world has always been a desperately dangerous place to live for the greater part of the earth's inhabitants; it was, however reluctantly, endured as the natural state of affairs. Yet the invention of every new weapon of war has always been greeted with horror and righteous indignation, especially by those who failed to invent it, or who were threatened with it first . . . bows and arrows, stone cannon balls, gunpowder, flintlocks, pistols, the dumdum bullet, the Maxim silencer, the machine gun, poison gas, armored tanks, and on and on to the grand climax—if it should prove to be—of the experiment on Hiroshima. Nagasaki was bombed too, remember? Or were we already growing accustomed to the idea? And as for Hiroshima, surely it could not have been the notion of sudden death of others that shocked us? How could it be, when in two great wars within one generation we have become familiar with millions of shocking deaths, by sudden violence of most cruel devices, and by agonies prolonged for years in prisons and hospitals and concentration camps. We take with apparent calmness the news of the deaths by millions by flood, famine, plague—no, all the frontiers of danger are down now, no one is safe, no one, and that, alas, really means all of us. It is our own deaths we fear, and so let's out with it and give up our fine debauch of moralistic frenzy over Hiroshima. I fail entirely to see why it is more criminal to kill a few thousand persons in one instant than it is to kill the same number slowly over a given stretch of time. If I have a choice, I'd as lief be killed by an atom bomb as by a hand grenade or a flame thrower. If dropping the atom bomb is an immoral act, then the making of it was too; and writing of the formula was a crime, since those who wrote it must have known what such a contrivance was good for. So, morally speaking, the bomb is only a magnified hand grenade, and the crime, if crime it is, is still murder. It was never anything else. Our protocriminal then was the man who first struck fire from flint, for from that moment we have been coming steadily to this day and this weapon and this use of it. What would you have advised instead? That the human race should have gone on sitting in caves gnawing raw meat and beating each other over the head with the bones?

And yet it may be that what we have is a world not on the verge of flying apart, but an uncreated one—still in shapeless fragments waiting to be put together properly. I imagine that when we want something better, we may have it: at perhaps no greater price than we have already paid for the worse.

# A VISIT TO AMERICA

## Dylan Thomas

Dylan Thomas (1914-1953), born in Carmarthenshire, Wales,
is best known as a poet who delights in a riotous, rhythmical
profusion of language. He also made a name for himself in
Britain as a radio broadcaster for the Welsh Region of the
British Broadcasting Corporation. The following essay, based
on Thomas' experiences in lecture tours to the United States
in 1950 and 1952, was recorded in 1953 before his final visit
to America. He died in New York in 1953, and the recorded
essay was broadcast the following year.

The essay first appeared in print in The Listener (April 22,
1954) and is reprinted from Quite Early One Morning
(1954).

Across the United States of America, from New York to California and back, glazed, again, for many months of the year there
streams and sings for its heady supper a dazed and prejudiced procession of European lecturers, scholars, sociologists, economists, writers,
authorities on this and that and even, in theory, on the United States
of America. And, breathlessly between addresses and receptions, in
planes and trains and boiling hotel bedroom ovens, many of these
attempt to keep journals and diaries. At first, confused and shocked
by shameless profusion and almost shamed by generosity, unaccus-
tomed to such importance as they are assumed, by their hosts, to
possess, and up against the barrier of a common language, they write
in their note-books like demons, generalizing away, on character and
culture and the American political scene. But, towards the middle of
their middle-aged whisk through middle-western clubs and universi-
ties, the fury of the writing flags; their spirits are lowered by the
spirit with which they are everywhere strongly greeted and which, in
ever-increasing doses, they themselves lower; and they begin to mis-
trust themselves, and their reputations—for they have found, too
often, that an audience will receive a lantern-lecture on, say, ceramics,

with the same uninhibited enthusiasm that it accorded the very week before to a paper on the Modern Turkish Novel. And, in their diaries, more and more do such entries appear as, "No way of escape!" or "Buffalo!" or "I am beaten," until at last they cannot write a word. And, twittering all over, old before their time, with eyes like rissoles in the sand, they are helped up the gangway of the home-bound liner by kind bosom friends (of all kinds and bosoms) who boister them on the back, pick them up again, thrust bottles, sonnets, cigars, addresses into their pockets, have a farewell party in their cabin, pick them up again, and, snickering and yelping, are gone: to wait at the dockside for another boat from Europe and another batch of fresh, green lecturers.

There they go, every spring, from New York to Los Angeles: exhibitionists, polemicists, histrionic publicists, theological rhetoricians, historical hoddy-doddies, balletomanes, ulterior decorators, windbags, and bigwigs and humbugs, men in love with stamps, men in love with steaks, men after millionaires' widows, men with elephantiasis of the reputation (huge trunks and teeny minds), authorities on gas, bishops, best sellers, editors looking for writers, writers looking for publishers, publishers looking for dollars, existentialists, serious physicists with nuclear missions, men from the B.B.C. who speak as though they had the Elgin Marbles [1] in their mouths, potboiling philosophers, professional Irishmen (very lepri-corny [2]), and I am afraid, fat poets with slim volumes. And see, too, in that linguaceous [3] stream, the tall monocled men, smelling of saddle soap and club arm-chairs, their breath a nice blending of whisky and fox's blood, with big protruding upper-class tusks and county moustaches, presumably invented in England and sent abroad to advertise Punch,[4] who lecture to women's clubs on such unlikely subjects as "The History of Etching in the Shetland Islands." And the brassy-bossy men-women, with corrugated-iron perms,[5] and hippo hides, who come, self-announced, as "ordinary British housewives," to talk to rich minked chunks of American matronhood about the iniquity of

[1] The Elgin Marbles are a famous collection of Greek statuary, now in the British Museum, brought to England (1803-1812) by Lord Elgin.
[2] Thomas' formation on leprechaun and corny.
[3] Thomas' formation on the root lingui- and the suffix -aceous.
[4] British humor magazine.
[5] Permanent waves (British slang).

the Health Services,[6] the criminal sloth of the miners, the *visible* tail and horns of Mr. Aneurin Bevan,[7] and the fear of everyone in England to go out alone at night because of the organized legions of cosh boys [8] against whom the police are powerless owing to the refusal of those in power to equip them with revolvers and to flog to ribbons every adolescent offender on any charge at all. And there shiver and teeter also, meek and driven, those British authors unfortunate enough to have written, after years of unadventurous forgotten work, one bad novel which became enormously popular on both sides of the Atlantic. At home, when success first hit them, they were mildly delighted; a couple of literary luncheons went sugar-tipsy to their heads, like the washing sherry served before those luncheons; and perhaps, as the lovely money rolled lushly in, they began to dream in their moony writers' way, of being able to retire to the country, keep wasps (or was it bees?), and never write another lousy word. But in come the literary agent's triggermen and the publisher's armed narks: [9] "You must go to the States and make a Personal Appearance. Your novel is *killing* them over there, and we're not surprised either. You must go round the States lecturing to women." And the inoffensive writers, who've never dared lecture anyone, let alone women—they are frightened of women, they do not understand women, they write about women as creatures that never existed, and the women lap it up—these sensitive plants cry out: "But what shall we lecture about?"

"The English Novel."

"I don't read novels."

"Great Women in Fiction."

"I don't like fiction or women."

But off they're wafted, first class, in the plush bowels of the Queen *Victoria* with a list of engagements long as a New York menu or a half-hour with a book by Charles Morgan,[10] and soon they are losing

---

[6] Health Services in Britain are administered by the government and paid for largely through taxes.

[7] Aneurin Bevan (1897-     ), Member of Parliament since 1929 from Monmouthshire, Wales, and radical Labourite, made headlines almost daily in the 1940's for his heated criticism of Prime Minister Churchill's policies, of "American reactionaries," and of his own party.

[8] Young toughs armed with clubs or bats (British slang).

[9] Informers, stool pigeons (British slang).

[10] Charles Morgan (1894-1958), minor novelist of Welsh descent.

their little cold-as-goldfish paw in the great general glutinous hand-shake of a clutch of enveloping hostesses. I think, by the way, that it was Ernest Raymond, the author of *Tell England*, who once made a journey round the American women's clubs, being housed and entertained at each small town he stopped at by the richest and largest and furriest lady available. On one occasion he stopped at some little station, and was met, as usual, by an enormous motor-car full of a large hornrimmed business man, looking *exactly* like a large hornrimmed business man on the films—and his roly-poly pearly wife. Mr. Raymond sat with her in the back of the car, and off they went, the husband driving. At once, she began to say how utterly delighted she and her husband and the committee were to have him at their Women's Literary and Social Guild, and to compliment him on his books. "I don't think I've ever, in all my life, enjoyed a book so much as *Sorrel and Son*," she said. "What you don't know about human nature! I think Sorrel is one of the most beautiful characters ever portrayed."

Ernest Raymond let her talk on, while he stared, embarrassed, in front of him. All he could see were the three double chins that her husband wore at the back of his neck. On and on she gushed in praise of *Sorrel and Son* until he could stand it no longer. "I quite agree with you," he said. "A beautiful book indeed. But I'm afraid I didn't write *Sorrel and Son*. It was written by an old friend of mine, Mr. Warwick Deeping."

And the large hornrimmed double-chinned husband at the wheel said without turning: "Caught again, Emily."

See the garrulous others, also, gabbing and garlanded from one nest of culture-vultures to another: people selling the English way of life and condemning the American way as they swig and guzzle through it; people resurrecting the theories of surrealism for the benefit of remote parochial female audiences who did not know it was dead, not having ever known it had been alive; people talking about Etruscan pots and pans to a bunch of dead pans and wealthy pots in Boston. And there, too, in the sticky thick of lecturers moving across the continent black with clubs, go the foreign poets, catarrhal troubadours, lyrical one-night-standers, dollar-mad nightingales, remittance-bards from at home, myself among them booming with the worst.

Did we pass one another, *en route*, all unknowing, I wonder, one of us, spry-eyed, with clean, white lectures and a soul he could call his own, going buoyantly west to his remunerative doom in the great State University factories, another returning dog-eared as his clutch of poems and his carefully typed impromptu asides? I ache for us both. There one goes, unsullied as yet, in his Pullman pride, toying, oh boy, with a blunderbuss bourbon, being smoked by a large cigar, riding out to the wide open spaces of the faces of his waiting audience. He carries, besides his literary baggage, a new, dynamic razor, just on the market, bought in New York, which operates at the flick of a thumb, but cuts the thumb to the bone; a tin of new shaving-lather which is worked with the other, unbleeding, thumb and covers not only the face but the whole bath-room and, instantly freezing, makes an arctic, icicled cave from which it takes two sneering bell-boys to extract him; and, of course, a nylon shirt. This, he dearly believed from the advertisements, he could himself wash in his hotel, hang to dry overnight, and put on, without ironing, in the morning. (In my case, no ironing was needed, for, as someone cruelly pointed out in print, I looked, anyway, like an unmade bed.)

He is vigorously welcomed at the station by an earnest crew-cut platoon of giant collegiates, all chasing the butterfly culture with net, note-book, poison-bottle, pin, and label, each with at least thirty-six terribly white teeth, and is nursed away, as heavily gently as though he were an imbecile rich aunt with a short prospect of life, into a motor-car in which, for a mere fifty miles or so travelled at poet-breaking speed, he assures them of the correctness of their assumption that he is half-witted by stammering inconsequential answers in an over-British accent to the genial questions about what international conference Stephen Spender [11] might be attending at the moment or the reactions of British poets to the work of a famous American whose name he did not know or catch. He is then taken to a small party of only a few hundred people all of whom hold the belief that what a visiting lecturer needs before he trips on to the platform is just enough martinis so that he can trip off the platform as well. And, clutching his explosive glass, he is soon contemptuously dismissing, in a flush of ignorance and fluency, the poetry of those

---

[11] Stephen Spender (1909-    ), English poet and lecturer.

androgynous literary ladies with three names who produce a kind of verbal ectoplasm to order as a waiter dishes up spaghetti—only to find that the fiercest of these, a wealthy huntress of small, seedy lions (such as himself), who stalks the middle-western bush with ears and rifle cocked, is his hostess for the evening. Of the lecture he remembers little but the applause and maybe two questions: "Is it true that the young English intellectuals are *really* psychological?" or, "I always carry Kierkegaard [12] in my pocket. What do you carry?"

Late at night, in his room, he fills a page of his journal with a confused, but scathing, account of his first engagement; summarizes American advanced education in a paragraph that will be meaningless to-morrow, and falls to sleep where he is immediately chased through long, dark thickets by a Mrs. Mabel Frankincense Mehaffey, with a tray of martinis and lyrics.

And there goes the other happy poet bedraggedly back to New York which struck him all of a sheepish never-sleeping heap at first but which seems to him now, after the ulcerous rigours of a lecturer's spring, a haven cosy as toast, cool as an icebox, and safe as skyscrapers.

---

[12] Søren Kierkegaard (1813-1855), Danish philosopher and theologian, whose work has lately become fashionable among young intellectuals.

# ON EDUCATION

## J. B. Priestley

J. B. Priestley was born in 1894 in Bradford in the West
Riding of Yorkshire. As he tells us in this essay, he served
in World War I and received a government grant to study
at Trinity Hall, Cambridge. He had been writing articles
and essays since 1910 and quickly acquired a reputation as
a reviewer, critic, dramatist, essayist, and novelist. He has
also been a director of the inflential New Statesman and
Nation, a radio lecturer and commentator, and an author of
plays for television.

This essay appeared originally in the New Statesman and
Nation (April 17, 1954) and is reprinted from Thoughts in
the Wilderness (1957).

When I was sixteen I left school and found myself a job in a wool
office. I had no intention of settling down in the wool business; I
had already made up my mind to be a writer, and indeed was already
writing hard; but clearly there was no living to be made out of
writing for some years to come, so into the office I went. That I was
allowed to remain there until I joined the army in 1914 is a tribute
to my personality, which then, if not now, was a peculiar mixture of
the insufferable and the enchanting; for there cannot have been many
young clerks worse than I was in the long history of the wool trade.
After about four and a half years in the army I received an ex-officer's
grant that took me to Cambridge but by no means kept me there,
even on a diet of bread and cheese and boiled eggs, so that I had to
eke out with journalism, coaching, odd lectures, anything to earn a
guinea or two. Finally, I left Cambridge for London, with some
vague introductions and capital of about forty-seven pounds.

Looking back, I can see quite clearly now that the great formative period for me was neither school nor the Cambridge years. It
was 1911-14, when nobody was trying to educate me nor paying for
me to be instructed, when, in fact, I was working (though as little as

possible) in the wool office. Our hours then were longer than most office hours are now: we had to be there at nine, took an hour for lunch, and usually finished sometime between six and seven. (If we worked after seven we received sixpence for tea money. No refreshment was provided before then.) We still sat on high stools like Dickens characters, and I was adroit at looking as if I were entering up the bag book, on my high desk, when in fact I was reading the poems of Yeats or Chesterton's last essays, lying inside my open drawer, which could be closed in a flash. I could also make a slower journey to and from the Bradford Conditioning House, losing myself in daydreams, than anybody else in the trade. Nevertheless, in spite of all these dodges, the office claimed me all the week and never let me go on Saturday until about half-past one. Nor did I live just round the corner from it, for our house, on the edge of the town, was at least two miles away. The fact remains, however, that this was the time when I learnt most and came along fastest. The State was not investing a penny in me.

(And here, for the benefit of those readers who believe in the State but not much in me, let me strike a rough balance. What have I had from the State? A very modest contribution towards my childhood and early youth, a grant that barely kept me alive at Cambridge, and a few fees for jobs undertaken from a sense of duty. What has it had from me? Fortunes in direct and indirect taxation, in Entertainment Tax on my plays and films, in foreign currency it badly needed, to say nothing about my services as a fighting soldier (no great shakes) in one war and as a day-and-night propagandist in another war. And if I should now go broke and dotty, I might receive with luck a Civil List pension of about two hundred a year. That is, if the country can afford it after meeting so many claims upon its generosity. I would have been ten times better off under George the Fourth).

The truth is, I was fortunate during those years in my environment. My native city of Bradford is frequently mentioned, mostly by people who know nothing about it, as a kind of symbol of "muck and brass," a stronghold of North-country narrow provincialism. But when I lived there, as a youth, it was considered the most progressive city in the Kingdom. It was a Labour outpost. The first elementary school in the country where meals were provided was the one of which my father was headmaster. We had a Labour weekly to which, during this period, I contributed a regular page. Moreover, a number of Liberal German-Jewish families had settled there, as in Manchester, to give our West Riding dough a leaven of culture. Our Subscription Concerts followed the same plan as those at Leipzig. We also had our Permanent Orchestra and two great Choral Societies. We had three local daily papers as well as several weeklies. We had two theatres and two music-halls. We had a flourishing Arts Club and a Playgoers' Society. Our Central Lending and Reference Libraries were excellent. Bradford men were making their names in the arts and sciences. And though the town was ugly enough, the inviolable moors, where we walked and talked most week-ends, began only a tuppenny tram-ride away. For a few pence more, taking a train, you reached the Dales, the most beautiful countryside in England.

So there we were, walking towards our vast sevenpenny teas, arguing over our pipes of fourpenny Navy Cut, listening to Nikisch and Busoni, Casals and Kreisler,[1] for ninepence, seeing Little Tich and Grock [2] for fourpence, reading H. M. Tomlinson in the local paper and Chesterton's Saturday essay in the *Daily News*, buying our shilling classics or Nelson's old sevenpenny series. I am not growling and grumbling again. For all I know to the contrary, lots of youngsters in their late teens are having as good a life now. Here I am not contrasting two periods. I am explaining why, in my considered judgment, these years, when I was neither in school nor college, turned out the most rewarding years I ever knew. It was, I repeat, because I was fortunate in my environment. It was not that I went to the right sort of school, but that I was living in the right sort of town. (Of course it might not have been right for you, but it was right for me.) In theory no doubt it was all wrong that a "gifted youth" should spend his best years working long hours in a wool office. In practice it worked well. But it worked well, not because I happened to have massive determination and an iron will

[1] Internationally famous musicians: Arthur Nikisch (1855-1922), Hungarian pianist and conductor; Ferruccio Busoni (1866-1924), Italian pianist and composer; Pablo Casals (1876-    ), Spanish cellist and composer; and Fritz Kreisler (1875-    ), Austrian violinist and composer.
[2] Two of the cleverest comedians of modern times: Little Tich (Harry Relph, 1868-1928), impersonator and dancer; Grock (Adrien Wettach, 1880-1959), Swiss clown.

(I have never had either at any time), but because there was something in the atmosphere of that place at that period which encouraged me to develop and to grow. I do not think any school or college, by itself, could have done it. I would always have been wondering what was happening outside the walls. I would have been telling myself that this scholastic seclusion was not real life. I would not have taken anybody's word about what was going on in the outer world. But living as I did, I knew I was experiencing real life, exploring the outer world, taking what I wanted from my own town. Thus I was educating myself.

Let us take a look at what seem at first sight to be more formal processes of education. For example, at Oxford and Cambridge. In what lies their unique value? I would reply without hesitation that it lies in their successful creation (not quite what it used to be, perhaps) of an atmosphere of disinterested scholarship, an environment in which thought itself is triumphant. A young man can live for at least nine terms in a place that does not care a damn about the price of cotton and tin and the export trade. He can sit up all night arguing about God and Art. He can lock himself in, as I did once, with a tin of tobacco, a case of beer, and the whole of the Elizabethan Drama. In such places knowledge is in the very air. Not the formal courses of instruction but the atmosphere and the surroundings enrich the student. I have long thought it a shame that our students of music and acting have to live in London, lost among millions who care little or nothing for these arts. They would do much better if, as sometimes happens abroad, they received instruction in some place where the very landladies and bus drivers had a passion for music or the theatre, where the street outside was the ally of the school.

Now we have to spend so much on the school that we cannot afford to civilise the street. We are hoping that sooner or later the school will be strong enough to overcome the street, that a generation of teenagers will finally leave school to tear down the street and rebuild the town. If you argue with enthusiastic educationalists, they will admit under pressure that so far the street seems to have won, but they will declare their faith in the imminent victory of the school. I wish I could share this faith. But the odds seem to me too heavily in favour of the street, the town, the local environment. If their influence is not good, then the good influence of the school will not last long. To nine youngsters out of ten, the values of their home, their street, their town, seem far more important than anything learnt at school. There, outside, is real life, the world of the adults, towards which they are headed, away from the kid stuff of the classrooms. So it is largely a waste of time and money trying to persuade children that Shakespeare is our pride and joy if the town they live in cannot even boast one theatre, and prefers the films of Abbott and Costello to all that Shakespeare ever wrote. And if more and more youngsters leaving school want to read the *Daily Scream,* which steadily gets worse and worse, then what return is our national investment in education bringing? No doubt we need more teachers and should offer them better prospects. But what guarantee have we that they can successfully challenge the proprietors of the *Daily Scream,* the TV, radio and film experts, the advertising gang, the haters of the arts, the slow murderers of eager, hopeful living? Who, so far, is winning all along the line?

But no, I must not growl and grumble. I will simply state the case, as I see it. I owe most to a time when I was not being formally educated but when I enjoyed an environment favourable to a youth of my sort. I realise that youth still has its opportunities, perhaps more of them in some directions than I had, but it does seem to me that by and large the environment is far less favourable than it was, chiefly owing to the recent development of mass communications and of what might be called a mass pseudo-culture. (Where comparison can be made, for example, with the popular Press, the decline is obvious.) Meanwhile, we spend more and more and more on Education, hoping rather desperately that somehow and sometime the values of the school will triumph over those of the streets outside the school. And this costs us so much that we cannot afford to change and improve the towns that receive our boys and girls after they have left school. The environment they know in their later teens, probably their most formative years, is a dreary mess of cheap commercial values, in which any fire kindled in the classroom is likely to be soon damped down and smothered. Perhaps the educationalists are right, and we have only to turn a corner. Perhaps I am an odd fish and cannot argue from my own experience. But I cannot help feeling thankful that I grew up before we had achieved such progress.

# TELEVIEWING

## J. B. Priestley

*See the preceding essay for biographical note.*
*This essay appeared originally in the* New Statesman and
Nation *(September 29, 1956) and is reprinted from* Thoughts
in the Wilderness *(1957).*

Down here on the island,[1] where I have rented a fine large set and
where we have a powerful transmitting mast not far away, I am a
Viewer. We keep the set in a room originally intended for music,
and I can sit in the dark there, viewing and viewing, without disturbing the rest of the household. I lie back in an armchair, put my
feet up on a stool, and smoke and view away. Except when there
are Test Matches,[2] I do all my viewing after dinner. Wheezing a bit,
heavy with food and drink, I waddle along the hall, switch on the
set, drop into my chair and put my feet up, then peer into my
magic mirror like a fourteen-stone cigar-smoking Lady of Shalott.[3]
At first I told myself that I watched the set and its antics for strictly
professional and technical reasons, but lately I have not had even a
shadow of that excuse. I am simply one of the Viewers. I have
already passed uncounted hours half-hypnotised by the jiggling and
noisy images. Sometimes I wonder if I am going out of my mind.
We have been told that the worst is over after about four years, but
long before that my outlook will have been so completely changed
that I shall be a different person. I shall probably be removed to
an old man's home. Let us hope these places are equipped with
good TV sets.

In my capacity as a Viewer, I have no intention of criticising

---

[1] The Isle of Wight.

[2] "Big-league" matches in cricket, often between international teams.

[3] The Lady of Shalott is a fairy maiden in Alfred Tennyson's narrative poem,
*Lady of Shalott* (1832), confined on an island and required by threat of a fatal
curse to gaze into a mirror and watch the "Shadows of the world appear."

adversely and in detail the way things are done. Given this strange medium and their own particular responsibilities, the people directing and handling the medium do almost all that can be reasonably expected of them. Most of them, I know, are enthusiasts; if removed from TV they would feel they were in exile. I don't imagine I could do it better myself. I think I would be far worse than they are. Most of the familiar jeers and sneers at their efforts seem to me quite unfair. The difficulties they have to face are too lightly disregarded. The critics who attack them make little or no allowance for the black magic of the medium itself, always discussing the entertainment provided as if they had not been staring at a set but sitting in a theatre, a cinema, a concert hall, a cabaret. So not a word that follows must be taken as unfriendly criticism of TV personnel. Good luck to you, boys and girls! Thanks a lot, Mary, Peter, Sylvia, Derek! But I am a Viewer too, one of the regular customers, even though I never ring up to complain that one of my precious prejudices has been ignored, and now I feel I must explain, as honestly as I know how, what the thing is doing to me.

The general line about TV—I took it myself before I became a Viewer—is that it is terrifically exciting, immensely powerful, potentially very dangerous. Here is this miraculous medium that pours into the home, hour after hour, night after night, images so dazzling and enticing that it immediately outbids all other media for its tenancy of the mind and imagination. It can transform any licence-holder [4] into a well-informed and thoughtful student of all public affairs. It can turn children into future scholars of Trinity and Girton [5] or into gunmen and molls. So we are playing with fire and dynamite—but what fire, what dynamite! This is the kind of stuff I wrote and talked myself before I became a real Viewer. Now that I know what happens, I can no longer write and talk in this strain. Certainly the medium produces its own particular effects, undoubtedly has an influence all its own; but these effects and this influence are very different from what they are generally imagined to be. Unless I am a very peculiar Viewer, the alarmists have all been looking in the wrong direction. They are like a man who expects a wolf

---

[4] Owners of television sets in Britain are required to purchase a license.
[5] Colleges of Cambridge University.

at the door when he ought to be attending to the death watch beetle in the woodwork.

Instal a set, turn a switch—and hey presto!—here in a corner of the living-room is an ever-changing image of the whole wide, glittering, roaring world. Or so they say. But that is not quite how my viewing works. To begin with, it does not seem to bring the outside world closer to me but pushes it further away. There are times, after I have played the Lady of Shalott longer than usual, when this world is not here at all; I feel I am taking a series of peeps, perhaps from the darkened smoke room of a giant spaceship, at another planet, with whose noisy affairs I am not involved at all. Let me stare and idly listen long enough and I seem to have arrived at some theosophical astral-body-life-after-death. I am as little involved in or perturbed by all these conferences, departures and arrivals of shadowy Ministers, crashes and floods, strikes and lockouts, aircraft and racing cars, atomic plants or fishing villages, scientists and film stars, as some Great White Master, a thousand years old, gazing into a crystal ball in Tibet. At most, these are—as one of Yeats's characters observed in another connection—the dreams the drowsy gods breathe on the burnished mirror of the world.[6] I remember an old retired nannie, rather weak in the head, who when she visited the silent films thought everything she saw was part of one vast confused programme, an astonishing but acceptable mixture of the Prince of Wales and cowboys and Indians and Stanley Baldwin and sinking ships and It-girls [7] and the Lord Mayor of London. She was an early Viewer. I know now exactly what she felt. Perhaps I am rather weak in the head too.

No sooner is any subject under review and discussion on the screen than it is drained of all reality. The instrument itself, probably guided by some satanic intelligence hostile to our species, adds a fatal dream effect. Even what I thought were urgent burning problems stop being problems at all. They are not settled, but their hash is. Somehow I no longer care what happens about Oil or Married Women At Work or Youth And The Churches Today or What We Do With The Old People or Whither Britain. I just view

---

[6] Lines spoken by a character in the first version (1900) of *The Shadowy Waters,* a dramatic poem by the Irish poet and playwright, William Butler Yeats.

[7] Girls with sex appeal.

them. They might be bits from untidy and badly acted plays. Sometimes I don't know—and don't care—if the gesticulating image of a Foreign Minister belongs to a real Foreign Minister or to an actor in one of those political plays we are always having. Here on the screen the difference between Yugoslavia and Ruritania is hardly worth bothering about. After half-an-hour of The Future Of Our Fisheries or Africa At The Crossroads, the programme personalities, bursting with fisheries or Africa, stare accusingly at me and ask me what I propose to do about it. They might as well know now that, as a Viewer, I don't propose to do anything about it. After they have given me a final earnest look and asked their last question, I stare at the credit titles, listen dreamily to the end music, wonder idly why Malcolm Muggeridge looks handsomer on the screen than off, where Woodrow Wyatt has acquired his new haughty accent, light another pipe, and float into the next programme.

Perhaps it is *Picture Parade* or something of the sort, in which all the imbecilities of the film studio hand-outs and the fan magazines are given a kind of idiot dream life, especially—ah what golden moments!—in the foyer at a gala première where celebrities of screen and stage consent to smile at us and tell us how exciting it all is, as if we didn't know, and are wished lots of luck. As a Viewer I try not to miss one of these occasions. To view one, smoking in the darkened room with your feet up, is much better than actually being there, what with all the dressing up, the heat and fuss, the pushing and shoving to get nearer the mike or the Press photographers. It is a dream glimpse, carefully focused and timed, of a dream world. But it is all so *exciting*, as everybody keeps telling us Viewers. Perhaps that is why I so often find myself laughing—all alone, there in the dark—probably only a nervous excitement.

Some nights there seem to be dozens and dozens and dozens of people being interviewed, not just about films but about everything. We go all over the place—inside and outside Ministries, home and abroad, to airports and railway stations, to sports grounds and factories. The organisation of it all, the sheer technical achievements, are a credit to our civilisation. The courtesy and friendliness are admirable: all the persons interviewed are for ever being thanked and wished good luck. People under Cabinet rank and sixty years of age are on Christian name terms at once. It is a wonderful and happy world, this of TV interviews. And perhaps that is why it is not a world in which anybody ever says anything. That might spoil it. Between the cordial *Hellos* and the charming *Good-byes* nothing much seems to happen. We are either going to the interview or coming away from it. "Let us," they say proudly, "go to Coketown and talk to the Mayor himself—so now *It's Over To Coketown*— This is Coketown and here in the studio is the Mayor of Coketown, who has kindly consented to talk to us—Very good of you, Mr. Mayor —er what about this er campaign of yours, Mr. Mayor?—Well, Reg, I think er I can say er we here in Coketown er hope to get it started fairly soon—Thank you, Mr. Mayor, and the best of luck—Thank you, Reg—And now we return you to London—This is London and that was the Mayor of Coketown being interviewed by our representative, Reg Rowbottom—and *now*——"

At first, when I was a new Viewer, a stranger in this magic world, I wanted the Mayor to say something, if only to justify all the trouble that had been taken to flash his image across the country. Now I know that this does not matter at all, that what is important is that we should keep jumping around, stare at a fresh face for a moment or two, then be off again. The instrument likes to do this, and it is the instrument that has us in its power. In this world of the magic tube, all the values are different. Here we are more interested in what the interviewer sounds and looks like than we are in what the interviewed person says. Viewing, I accept these topsy-turvy values. It is only afterwards, coming to my senses and thinking things over, I begin to question them. Staring at the set, my mind almost a blank, I am quite ready to believe in TV personalities, the élite and aristocracy of this dream world. I do not ask what they have done, what massive talents they possess. They still have personalities where I, as a Viewer, a captive of the screen, have little or none. Not this Christmas but possibly the next, when I may have said good-bye to reality, I shall have no party of my own, perhaps will no longer understand what arrangements could be made for one; I will attend, as a Viewer, a party of TV personalities, to enjoy the sparkle of the wine in their glasses, to listen with joy to the crunching of their mince pies; and one or two of them may look straight in my direction, to wish me a Merry Christmas Programme, a Happy New Year's Viewing.

Meanwhile, sitting in the dark with my feet up, I feel I have *had* Fisheries or Africa or Youth And The Churches Today. I couldn't agree more about Married Women At Work or What We Do With The Old People or Whither Britain, and could hardly care less. We Viewers know now that we are such stuff as dreams are made on,[8] that all is Maya,[9] that *For in and out, above, below, 'Tis nothing but a magic shadow-show.*[10] So it is easy to imagine oneself viewing the next war, dreamily watching whole cities crumble to radioactive dust, catching a last glimpse of Manchester or Leeds in between a thirty-minute detective play and some light music and a gipsy dancer. Never did a medium of information and entertainment arrive more opportunely, to soothe the tormented mind, to ease the bewilderment of the soul. We may emerge from our four or five years' bondage to it, having at last achieved detachment, for ever untroubled and smiling, finally victorious over the technique and the instrument. Already we Viewers, when not viewing, have begun to whisper to one another that the more we elaborate our means of communication, the less we communicate. Some words on a page can be unforgettable. The memory of an actor, moving, and speaking on a platform, may haunt us all our lives. Then the inventors and technicians arrive, the costs rise prodigiously, the complication sets in, and we get film and radio, far less potent and memorable. The inventors and technicians, in a frenzy, with millions of money behind them, invade the home with TV, adding more and more images to sound, performing miracles with time and space, bringing in colour, stereoscopic sight, everything. And out of this mountain of invention and technique, finance and organisation, comes a little dream mouse. "Not bad," we Viewers cry. "What next?"

---

[8] *The Tempest*, IV.i.156-157.
[9] In Hindu philosophy, illusion, vanity, or deceptive appearance.
[10] The lines are taken from stanza 46 of the first edition (1859) of Edward Fitzgerald's translation of *The Rubáiyát* of Omar Khayyám.